The PERILS *and* FORTUNE *of the* DUKE *of* OSUNA

Don Mariano Téllez-Girón and Beaufort, Twelfth Duke of Osuna

The PERILS *and* FORTUNE *of the* DUKE *of* OSUNA

ANTONIO MARICHALAR

Translated from the Spanish by
HARRIET de ONIS

ILLUSTRATIONS

Quand je luis je me consume.---Joubert

J. B. LIPPINCOTT COMPANY
Philadelphia & London

Manufactured in the
United States of America

To She Might Have Been

CONTENTS

PART I

PART II

PART III

PART IV

CONTENTS

PART V

PART VI

ILLUSTRATIONS

Part One

"NOT EVEN OSUNA!"

I. A DASHING DEVIL-MAY-CARE LOT

The Girón family is two hundred and forty-three years older than the Ottoman empire of the Turks which enjoys so much majesty and power in the world today, for their reign did not begin until 1306.

HIERONYMUS GUDIEL

THE first name in Spain," says General Fernández de Córdoba, speaking, in his *Memoirs*, of his contemporary Osuna.

"You'd think he was Osuna," repeats, afterwards, the populace of Madrid, to whom this name had become the symbol of generosity and splendour.

Osuna is the one jewel in the rubbish heap. Spain is crumbling to pieces at this time; the streets are alleys, hallways are caves, street-lights, mere glimmers; revolutions are only riots; war, but guerrilla-fighting, and the great fortunes are reckoned in farthings and sixpence. But there is a certain longing for grandeur in a people that continues to starch its percale until it can stand alone, shoes itself in patent leather, and can find money to pay a coiffeur to wave and pomade its hair, and which seeks a patron saint that shall incarnate its own generosity and nobility.

And so it builds up this legend: a baroque niche to enshrine the capricious image of a dashing aristocrat, his breast a "tatter of blood and gold."

Well set-up, inclined to be corpulent and very erect is Don Mariano Girón, small of foot, slender of waist, and with a delicate, plump hand. He carries his head very high and wears his hair combed forward over his temples. He is the spirited, devil-may-care, lavish gallant who runs through the greatest fortune so it shall not be said that anybody else could eclipse him. Born in the palace of Vistillas, brought up by servants, loved and understood by the people—for class hostility becomes virulent only between contingent groups—Osuna is never the Crœsus who traffics in mortgages and interest, "the rich man whose money," as Rivarol says, "brings him only the fear of losing it." Osuna is the lord of Vistillas, the lord of his street, the offspring of a race which contemplates its own image in him, and satisfies through him its own stifled longings. Neither gambler nor philanthropist, Osuna never spends merely to be spending; he spends because he feels that he is the cynosure of attention and under perpetual obligation; his role is that of the munificent hero, ever on duty. Osuna inherits an annual income of five million pesetas, and leaves, on his death, a deficit of forty-four million. He defies the lords of business with his overwhelming disdain. He burns his bridges and returns to the arms of his people; from the eminence of his white charger he shares his cloak with them, tearing to tatters once and for all the fabric his progenitors had alternately woven and rent.

The Giróns came by their arrogance honestly. One Rodrigo Girón, a son of the one who fought in the battle of Las Navas, was surrounded on his deathbed, in 1245, by two hundred and fifty-five knights, all of them his vassals, and during his lifetime, so his epitaph runs, he had over twelve hundred.

Rich in passions was the famous Knight Commander Don Pedro Girón, first lord of Ureña and Osuna, of whom it was said that "he was the bravest, the richest, and the most turbulent of all the nobles in Spain; he was respected like a king, and he laid down laws instead of obeying them; his post as Commander of his Order, his display, his bravery, his vast estates, and his very haughtiness made him the most renowned of all the grandees." He obtained the hand of her who was later to become Queen Isabel the Catholic, but so much against the will of his promised bride that she spent night and day on her knees, imploring death for herself or for her approaching bridegroom, and all the while Beatriz de Bobadilla hovered near, with unsheathed dagger, prepared to free her from the Commander if the death she so fervently besought dallied. But death came opportunely, overtaking the Commander on his way, at Villarrubia.

Rich, too, but in honourable accomplishments, was another Girón, Juan Téllez, fourth Count of Ureña. "A prince of singular virtue and exemplary piety," he was known to posterity as "the Saint." And even more than rich, opulent, were the others, and above all, the famous Don Pedro, the third duke, lauded by Quevedo, and called by history, "the Grand Duke of Osuna." The episodes of his much-discussed vice-regency are well known, his munificence, his style of living, his lavish display of arms and galleys, his gifts: ". . . To Uceda 200,000 ducats in coin, vases of silver enamelled with branches of orange and lemon which weighed one hundred and twenty-five pounds; three hundred fans of ivory and ebony; horses, trappings, damasquined scimitars and daggers; objects whose virtue resided more in the artifice of their construction than in the gold, rubies, diamonds and emeralds of which they were made, etc." Famous, likewise, for his Shaksperian administration of justice: to those who appropriated to their own use the estate of a minor, alleging that they were bound by law to give them "only that which they desired," he would say, "No, you have not interpreted the terms of the will correctly. It orders you to give the heir 'that which you desire'; now, what is it that you desire? The estate? Well, that is what you are to turn over to the heir. This is my command."

And like these, others and others . . . for "such has been the illustrious house of the Giróns that it has not merely maintained its brilliance and splendor . . . but has been enriched with brilliant and praiseworthy achievement, etc.," writes the author of the Chronicle of the Giróns in Alcalá, in 1577, adding: "and its antiquity is such that many of the notable and ancient things which the world bears in its memory exceed it but little in time and many of them are exceeded by it."

II. BENEATH THE GIRÓN MANTLE

Pour cimier, pour supports l'héraldique bétail,
Licorne, léopard, alérion ou guivre,
Monstres, géants captifs qu'un coup de vent délivre,
Exhaussent leur stature et cabrent leur poitrail.
J. M. DE HEREDIA

IT is not easy to get to Osuna. Embattled behind his shield he always interposes between himself and the public's curiosity, on palaces, carriages and liveries, his coat-of-arms, made up of a motley assemblage of the most aristocratic devices. It is supported by lions, surrounded by crosses, ribbons, and collars, and enshrouded in the purple mantle of the Grandee, heavy with decorations and lined with ermine:

L'hermine vierge de souillure
Qui, pour abriter leurs frissons,
Ouate de sa blanche fourrure
Les épaules et les blasons.

From the ducal coronet emerges the angel of Toledo habited and brandishing a sword with the motto: *Tu in ea et ego pro ea.* On one side the white charger of the Giróns and on the other the Pimentel eagle launch their battle-cries. On the face of the shield, quartered and conjoined, the lions of Silva, Ponce de León, and Enríquez, the Borja bull, the fish of Salm-Salm, the Estuñiga chains, the lilies of La Cerda and Arellano, the Guzmán cauldrons, the vorant Haro wolves, and turrets and panels, suns, stars, crescents, vairs and lozenges. And in the centre of this achievement *en ecuson*—or in the abyss, as the classics of heraldry call it—quartered with the pales of Beaufort, the Pimentel scallop shells, and the Mendoza ribands, and bordered by the Cisneros checky and Portuguese besants, the arms of the first Giróns display their red wound:

Y los Girónes tres de colorado
En el campo de oro, o de amarillo
Qu'encima dellos tienen al un lado
El león, y al otro, junto a él, el castillo;
Con escaques en torno arrodeado
De color de amapola y de membrillo
Los traen los de Girón, del que se halla
Que al Rey tomó el girón en la batalla.

Thus "Luys Çapata" in canto XXV of his *Carlo*

Famoso describes to the captive King Francis I the arms displayed in the Heraldic Hall of the Infantado Palace—afterward Osuna's—in Guadalajara.

Tradition has it that at the famous defeat on the Sagra, on October 23, 1086, the valiant Rodrigo de Cisneros—afterwards known as "the tattered"—saved the life of King Alfonso VII, giving him his horse and changing cloaks with him. He remained "on foot amidst the enemy fighting them back so bravely that the king was able to make his escape. He tore a three-cornered patch from the royal surcoat in commemoration of his exploit, and added Girón (*tatter*) to his name. The memory of this feat was preserved on his shield, "in poppy-red and quince-yellow" on a checky field.

Through this riven flank, down the insatiable jaws of this gaping tear, the Girón patrimony disappeared time after time; it was so great that in spite of having been squandered away more than once by its heirs—and by the sovereigns who, on occasion, denied them their rights, to undermine their power—it was still the greatest fortune in Spain in the nineteenth century.

A bottomless pit, the house of Girón, an abyss—"which grows ever greater the more is taken from it"

—a trapdoor down which so much was thrown, and where eventually everything would go, today, with the male line of the Giróns extinct—and the direct succession to the Osuna title, which is strictly entailed—of its glory there remains but a solitary echo, as melancholy as the lament of the breakers on the shores of night.

III. A FIERY STEED

L'ambition est un cheval farouche que ne cesse de ruer jusqu'à qu'il ait mis son homme à bas.

AMYOT

NOTHING remains of Osuna; neither the name, nor the race, nor the fortune, nor its history, hardly a paper or a record. . . . A visitor of the time says "there was not a leaf" in the drives of the magnificent Alameda. Osuna always took care to efface his every vestige. History is made by footprints: a clear, unobscured trail admirably traced, but lifeless.

But he left a wake of a different sort. Looking up one discovers the feathery cloud of smoke of his legend: a plume of tenuous vapour, which presages, in its vague outlines, the forming waterspout, something that will overwhelm, overpower and blind.

Then the deluge, devastation, destruction, gale,

whirlwind. Only sparks remain of all his splendour, and of his passage upon the earth, only the shadow of a white steed in headlong flight.

From earliest times an untamed white charger, with roses between its teeth and broken reins, had reared itself aloft on the Girón shield. It wants to be the first—*Primus et ire viam* proclaims the warcry above its floating mane—and it plunges into space over the golden circlet that imprisons it. Where others had their better judgment, the Giróns had a white, runaway charger. The race was already launched on its mad career when the last Girón of the original line, the Duke Don Mariano, hurled himself into the abyss of his ruin amidst roses, and with loosened reins.

A curious coincidence: the Duke had in his palace a beautiful engraving by Jacet representing the famous scene from *Mazeppa.* Byron and Victor Hugo sang the romantic adventure of the hero who traversed the earth tied to a horse and pursued by wolves. Vernet put it on canvas.

Bound to and guided by the fiery charger of his diadem, Osuna likewise rushes on in wild flight. Savage beasts assail him, close in on him. The charger will save him; but the mantle of this new Mazeppa will be left in shreds and tatters on the briars.

Un cri part; et soudain voilà que par la plaine
Et l'homme et le cheval emportés, hors d'haleine,
Sur les sables mouvants
Seuls, emplissant de bruit un tourbillon de poudre,
Pareil au noir nuage où serpente la foudre,
Volent avec les vents.

IV. "BETTER TO FLY"

Who are these that fly as a cloud . . .
ISAIAH, LX, 8

To fly, to fly and never be overtaken," sang Stanislaus Wyspianski, the poet of the steppe. . . . Because the angels fly, because the apostles flew, because the birds fly, the Pimentels, Count-Dukes of Benavente, attempted to fly; and Osuna, as head of this line, crowned his coat-of-arms with the Pimentel eagle, and its ambitious cry: *Better to fly*. To fly, to reach the sun, to be suns themselves was the consuming passion of this proud, presumptuous race which dramatized itself and was consumed in the insatiable holocaust of its own passions.

"Reason is the historian, but the passions are the actors," said Rivarol. And side by side with the facts

"Better to Fly"

of history, Osuna played out for all time his own farce. Fourteen times a Grandee, fifty-two titles, four princedoms and the greatest fortune in Spain: of this a Téllez-Girón made a huge funeral pyre with which he dazzled his contemporaries. (At this same time the English æsthetes were striving to "make of life a work of art" with a few dead leaves in a glass and a pot of judiciously applied yellow paint.)

Osuna always used the white charger on his shield, the eagle and the "Better to fly"; but he also bore the unsheathed wings of the angel of Toledo, and as Count of Beaufort he had another eagle displayed above the bends, the bendlets, the garters and cotices which came to him from his mother.

This noble lady was Marie Françoise de Beaufort, who was born in Paris in 1785, Countess of Beaufort and of the Holy Roman Empire, eldest daughter of Frederick August, Duke, Count, and Marquis of Beaufort-Spontin, Marquis of Florennes, Viscount of Eclaye and Ocidenbourg and Baron of Hosden, Governor General of Belgium and Chamberlain of the Emperor of Germany. And the Duchess of Beaufort, Osuna's grandmother, was Maria de los Dolores Leopolda of Toledo and Salm-Salm, daughter and heiress of the twelfth Duke of Infantado, who added this house to those of her grandson Osuna, who was to send them all flying to the four winds.

V. A FAMILY OF FRILLS AND FURBELOWS

L'orgueil n'est pas un crime aux enfants de ma race.
C. DE BERGERAC

THE Dukes of Osuna were made grandees in the nineteenth century as Count-Dukes of Benavente and head of the house of Pimentel . . . "a famous crew." And if on the Girón side it came to them to be rowdy, sporting, and extravagant, their foppishness came from the Pimentels. The Pimentels were a race of impertinent, punctilious coxcombs, the cream of the most pretentious court circles: hothouse plants, shielded by their heraldic green mantle. They were the capricious dandies who, with no end of airs and whims, always tried to set themselves apart from their associates. They were cultured, exacting, insolent, overbearing, dissatisfied, and voluble, and the slightest offence to their self-esteem flicked them on the raw.

The grandmother and guardian of our Duke of Osuna was a Pimentel, Maria Josefa de la Soledad Alonso-Pimentel, Téllez-Girón, Borja and Centellas, Countess-Duchess of Benavente and Duchess of Bejar, Arcos, Gandia, etc., in her own right, and "the lady of highest degree in Spain, and the most elegant and aristocratic in Europe," the patroness of Iriarte, of Don Ramón de la Cruz, of the bull-fighter Romero, of Goya, and the rival of the famous Duchess of Alba, Cayetana. She built the Alameda, which she called "My Caprice," and had it decorated by Goya and reproduced with her monogram on her fan.

There is no end to the stories about this lady. One day a certain ambassador, whose supply of champagne had run short the last time he entertained, went to call on her, and when his horses were unhitched in the stables of the Alameda buckets of champagne were brought to water them.

A well-known but improbable anecdote is also attributed to her. She was playing one night at a gaming table; somebody dropped a coin on the floor and stopped the game to look for it. Whereupon the Duchess illuminated the search with a handful of notes she

Maria Josefa Pimentel, Grandmother and Guardian of the Eleventh Duke of Osuna

lighted over the candles. No, the arrogant impulses of the Duchess were not easily restrained. She slashed four knife thrusts through the portrait Esteve painted of her, and Goya revenged himself for the respect he had been obliged to observe in his canvases, by making her the subject of many of his satirical drawings.

A sincere heart, Baudelaire, has said: "The refined —*incroyables, beaux, lions* or *dandis*—all have the same origin, and all have in common their character of opposition and rebellion; they are all representative of the best in human pride." And one who listened carefully to the heart, Bourdalou, said: "*L'orgueil est l'endroit le plus vif du cœur; pour peu qu'on y touche, la douleur nous fait pousseur des hauts cris.*" And when honour goes hand in hand with pride?

The act of a certain rebellious, fire-eating Benavente is famous, and the Duke of Rivas made it the subject of one of his ballads. The action takes place in Toledo. The Count of Benavente has refused to receive the faithless Duke of Bourbon in his palace. The latter complains to the Emperor. Charles V issues his orders. The Count obeys the command but says to the Emperor:

THE DUKE OF OSUNA

You are my sovereign on earth
My life and my possessions
Are all yours to command.

Your vassal am I, and my house,
And both are at your orders;
But lay no finger on my honor
And respect my conscience.

Let Bourbon lodge in my house,
Since such is your will,
Let him contaminate its walls,
Let him degrade its honors.

Toledo will give me shelter
Without having to rub shoulders
In my own house with traitors
Whose very breath is pestilent.

And as soon as he departs
Before I cross my threshold
I shall purify with fire
The walls which covered him.

* * * * *

Even today a few old walls
Blackened with smoke and time
Recall this glorious action
Which happened in famous Toledo.

Part Two

THE INTERLUDE OF DON PEDRO THE FRUSTRATED

VI. AT MONTRESOR'S COURT

That beautiful pale face is my fate.
CAROLINE LAMB

A QUIVERING vibrates through space: a tremolo begins very deep, rises, peals forth, and finally dies away. The first quarter of the nineteenth century has come to an end, and everything is slowly turning pale. The air—embalmed in livid sighs—stirs gently, not to blast these first tender shoots of Romanticism. To the cream of Madrid society the high note in fashion is F sharp. It had been reached by Montresor, "an Italian tenor whose looks, voice and manners turned the head of every unwed maiden, and of many who were." The leading beauties of the day vie with each other to see him and have his eyeglass turned on them: the celebrated Paquita Urquijo, the lovely Montufar, the beautiful Villagarcia, the enchanting Heredias, Santa Cruzs, and Contaminas.

He owed his vogue to the cnthusiasm which everything that had to do with *bel canto* aroused at that time. The glasses of fashion at the court lost no time in following the styles which the opera star launched. "One of the most celebrated at this was the tenor Montresor. The gilded youth slavishly imitated the cut of his frockcoats, which were made with a little cape over the shoulders, and his overcoats and hats which were known as *à lo Montresor*. . . . This was Madrid, this its society . . . at the end of August of 1825." The quotation is from General Fernández de Córdoba.

Two by the clock of the convent of San Jeronimo. The fashionable hour for a stroll before lunch to work up an appetite. The leaders of fashion were usually late, due, beyond doubt, to the time spent before the mirror trying out what Brummel termed "our mistakes": rumpled knots of stubborn cravats that refused to comply with the rules of art as set forth in thick volumes, *à lo Byron, lazy style, à lo Talma, Jesuit style, Oriental style, Russian style, in cascade, in fountain, etc.* And not only the cravats: hats *à la Ourika,* redingotes in Pilgrim fashion, shoes *à la bombé* and *à la farolê,* capes *à lo Almaviva,* with scarlet velvet facings or gold. The Marquis of Lozoya adds other details concerning the picturesque nomenclature given to materials: lustrina, mazandran, oceanida, barabin, and the colours: nigger-head, frog in love, Vesuvian flame, Nubian sand, and spider meditating a crime.

The Prado, in this festive array, must have been a dazzling sight. A spectator describes it as "a magnificent and fascinating spectacle." The furs and embroideries, velvets, laces, diamonds and jewels which would seem showy and vulgar in a public place nowadays were then indispensable accessories for the most select and brilliant members of society. With these the dress uniforms must be imagined, turning back the rays of the sun with their gold, blue, and scarlet trimmings; the claw-hammer coats of almond green with their pearl grey trousers, the brittle patent-leather, the stiffly starched cone-shaped collars that reached to the curled sideburns, the silk hats, the chains and ornamented watch-fobs, the sabres, shakoes, dolmans, epaulettes, etc.; the click of the thoroughbred's hoofs as it pranced along guided by a white-gloved hand, the noise and murmur of the people, and the disagreeable creak of the heavy carriages as they rolled along drawn by glossy coated mules and driven by an old liveried coachman. To refresh the dust-laden atmosphere Neptune pours forth a spray from his watery chariot and with his iron trident and stone whiskers acts as presiding deity of the avenue; and Apollo, the golden-haired dandy of another age, high on his pedestal, surveys the crowd beneath him with a disdainful smile, similar, no doubt, to that he bestowed on the venomous Python in its death agony.

VII. THE FIRST VOICE

Triste de mi!

ESPRONCEDA

MOUNTED on a dappled grey, with fine prancing hoofs, alert ears, onyx eyes and dainty muzzle, there appears a young man, the pinnacle of the society of his day. Out of the fur collar of his Polish overcoat with its garnitures of silk cord, there emerges a pale face, crowned with fair curls. The blue eyes, at once yearning and disdainful, are submerged in some inner torment. He has detached himself from the aristocratic group which accompanies him—San Carlos, Frías, Corres, Pontejos, and Santiago—and, holding his silk hat in his hand he goes curvetting along beside an emblazoned carriage where rides the lady of his thoughts.

His silhouette disappears amidst the carriages, but not the memory of him.

He is in fact the most dashing gallant of the day; his charm, his accomplishments, his titles, and his fortune make him perhaps the best match in Europe; he is the Duke of Osuna, Don Pedro de Alcántara Téllez-Girón and Beaufort, "striking appearance, exquisite amiability and uncommon talent." General Córdoba goes on to describe the Duke's "gracious and attractive aristocratic and diplomatic manners . . . his palaces with their wealth of art treasures, family arms, rich armour, and the collections of paintings, books and manuscripts brought together by his ancestors, the twenty dukes of Osuna and Infantado" which were the talk of all Madrid at the time.

Don Pedro possessed ten grandeurs of Spain, and among other titles that of: First Voice in the Councils of the Estate of Nobles of Cerdeña, and this is what he was in Madrid: the first voice, for as if to crown the most esteemed graces and gifts of this period he had such a beautifully modulated voice, and so well trained, that it was the delight of all who had the good fortune to hear him. He had probably inherited his musical vocation from his paternal grandmother, who

Don Pedro de Alcántara Téllez-Girón and Beaufort,
Eleventh Duke of Osuna

was a great patroness of these arts, and from her lovely daughters, who have come down to posterity each with the attribute of her particular gift. "Aunt Josefa," the Marchioness of Camarasa, was painted at the piano by Augustín, and Goya painted Manuela, the Duchess of Abrantes, holding a sheet of music and Joaquina, the Marchioness of Santa Cruz, with a lyre in her hand.

After studying music and particularly the organ, Don Pedro cultivated his voice with enthusiasm and ability under Valldemosa, who taught him to place it properly, beneath the firm clasp of the most exquisite of neckcloths. "His voice was a baritone or lyric bass; his technique was superb and he gave great feeling and colour to the phrases of the selection he was singing, in keeping with the type of music and the part he was interpreting."

Like the legitimate Osuna that he was he carried an opera star within him: he adored the *bel canto,* he dressed *à lo Montresor,* combed his hair *à la Cortessi,* and when the famous Rubini, who wrung tears from the public in *Perché no posso odiarti* from *La Sonambula* came to Madrid, Osuna "lodged him in his own palace and treated him like a prince."

In the drawing-rooms he sang impassioned duets

with his cousin and sweetheart, Encarnación Camarasa who, by all reports, was the loveliest girl and had the most beautiful voice in the court.

Over the fair, beautifully curled head of Don Pedro de Alcantara Téllez-Girón, the seventh of this name, in the transcourse of his splendid, ephemeral existence, the Goddess of Fortune was pleased to pour out the riches of her horn again and again. And yet he was Don Pedro the Frustrated. Everything smiled upon him, but he, did he ever smile, perchance? In the midst of his opulent splendour he suffered the pangs of an overpowering love. For this he lived and in this he found a beautiful death. Osuna was the embodiment of the Romanticism of the epoch, and he owed it to himself to be unhappy. A true-born gentleman, he kept the faith even to the point of imposing it cruelly upon his own destiny.

Bethencourt says of him that "he outshone everyone with his elegance, pomp and charm," and Saldoni called him the "father and protector of artists," on whom he bestowed lavish pensions so they could complete their studies abroad. He kept up the chapel with nine chaplains and musicians which another Count Ureña, a devoté of music like himself, had founded in Osuna. He acquired paintings, beautified his parks and his palaces; at his banquets verses were recited and he carried his devotion to the Muses to the point of having a bard for his sponsor when he covered his curly head before Fernando VII.

On July 7, 1830, when, as Count-Duke of Benavente, he received the grandee's privilege of appearing covered in the king's presence, he was presented by a man whose ability was in inverse ratio to his aspirations: the Duke of Frías, who had indited inspired stanzas *To the first steam-boat that made the voyage from Cadiz to Barcelona,* and who had written such popular compositions as: *The tears of the exile, Ode to Industry and the Arts,* in addition to funeral odes, odes in the heroic manner, epithalamiums, etc., and who years afterward was awarded a gold medal by Isabel II, on the occasion of a brilliant literary contest in the Artistic and Literary Lyceum of Madrid.

It was the Duke Don Pedro Alcántara de Osuna himself who at this time presided over and lent support to this Artistic and Literary Lyceum—peace to its ashes! It was, as Esquivel has painted it, the gathering ground of Romanticism's artists and writers, and one and the other aroused the enthusiasm of the ladies and gentlemen who were anybody in the Madrid of that day. The Lyceum which had been founded in 1837 was growing rapidly, thanks to the support of writers and artistocrats and bankers like Remisa and Salamanca who "generously opened their coffers to maintain the society's splendour." When it was installed in Atocha street, with the Duke of Osuna at its head, it developed rapidly under his direction. Somewhat later the Marquis of Valmar described it to his nephew, the Duke of Rivas, in telling him, among other things, about the first daguerreotype seen in Madrid: "The Lyceum was the haunt of pleasant cordiality and delicate culture. . . . The Romantic movement in arts and letters, whose extravagances were not clearly understood at the time, acted as a link between the most varied classes of cultivated society. Exclusive and aristocratic ladies and the leaders of wealth and power spent hours of recreation and enjoyment there in the company of other ladies of modest station and unknown youths who sought glory with their brush or their pen in that privileged circle. Snobbishness had not yet been invented . . . and people flocked to the Lyceum for the sole purpose of hearing the ballads of your father, the Andalusian scenes of Rubí, the poems of Espronceda and Vega, the legends and songs of Hartzenbusch, Gertrudis Avellaneda, etc."

VIII. A GALLANT YOUTH

. . . aquel delirio
aquella fiebre de amante,
abrasadora, incesante,
que más que gozo es martirio
VENTURA DE LA VEGA

IT was by chance that he saw the clear white light of day in Cadiz on September 10, 1810. His grandmother, Duchess of Arcos as well as of Benavente, had holdings there. He was baptized the same day, being carried to the font by this same grandmother, Doña María Josefa, who trailed her pompous brocades over the cold stones of the military chapel. He soon came to Madrid. He was raised in the Alameda, and in the palace on Leganitos street where the Dukes of Osuna had an important public library. He was very fond of the arts and literature; so much so that, although he became a good swordsman and a skilled rider, the tranquil pleasures of the mind, as opposed to the bellicose ardours which had burned in so many of his ancestors, and were already beginning to glow in his younger brother Mariano, were always predominant in him.

Perhaps the only mission in life of this ill-starred Don Pedro Girón, the frustrated, was—during his few brief years—to charm the ladies and inherit, one after another, the most noble and powerful titles in Spain. While but a child, in 1820, he succeeded to the titles of his father, in addition to the marquisate of Peñafiel, to which his primogeniture entitled him. The earldom of Ureña, which was older than the dukedom, went with it; the earldom of Fontanar, the title of grandee of the first order, and the offices of First Notary of Castile and First Gentleman of the Bedchamber, hereditary in his family, as well as the suzerainty of the towns of Morón de la Frontera, Arahar, Cazalla de la Sierra, Archidona, Olvera, Ortejicar, Tiedra, Briones and Gumiel de Izán which had come down through many entailments. In 1835, on the death of his grandmother and godmother, he became Count and Duke of Benavente, Duke of Bejar, of Plasencia, of Gandia, of Arcos, of Monteagudo, of Mandas and

Villanueva; Prince of Squilache; Marquis of Gibraleón, of Lombay, of Zahara, and of Terranova (which he ceded to his brother and heir Don Mariano); Count of Mayorga, of Bañares, of Belalcazar, of Oliva, of Mayalde; Viscount of Puebla and Alcocer; First Voice in the Councils of the Estate of Nobles of Cerdeña, and Chief Justice of Castile, overlord of numerous dependencies, and he was the head of such houses as Alonso-Pimentel, Borja, Ponce de Léon, Zuñiga, etc. And as though this were not enough, on November 27, 1841, on the death of his uncle, the impressive Don Pedro of Toledo and Salm-Salm, he succeeded to the possessions of the house of Mendoza, which included the duchies of Infantado, Lerma, Medina de Rioseco, Pastrana, Estremera, Francavila; he became Prince of Eboli and Mélito; Marquis of Santillana, Cenete, Tavara, Almenara, Argüeso, Algecilla and Cea; Count of Real de Manzanares, Saldaña, Cid, Villada, and Melgar; also Master of the Hunt of Seville, Knight of Calatrava, Grand Cross and Collar of the order of Carlos III, member of the Legion of Honour, etc.

He was also acting Gentleman of the Bedchamber, and representative of the crown in the legislatures of

1834 and 1836, in both of which offices he acquitted himself with distinction. As representative of the First Estate, in the year '36 Osuna presented a motion for the suspension of the decrees authorizing the sale of property belonging to religious organizations. He headed a group of young aristocrats opposing Mendizabal, and with the support of Miraflores, Quesada, and the ambassador of France, they had the satisfaction of seeing their measure passed. But later on Osuna, together with other liberals—Veragua, Rivas, San Carlos, Toreno, Miraflores, Isturiz—was obliged to leave the country, and for a time his rich possessions were declared forfeit. As Gentleman-in-Waiting to Her Majesty it was he who, in the year '43, stopped and ejected from the antechamber that daring Olozaga, president of the assembly who, it was said at the time, had forcibly secured from the young Queen a decree of dissolution in that famous and improbable keyhole scene.

On Fernando VII's death Osuna had espoused his daughter's cause, and for this he was named Colonel of the second regiment of the militia of Madrid. The Duke refused to accept the appointment, and offered himself as a private, which was, in his opinion, the rank to which his merits entitled him. A little later, when the court was transferred to Aranjuez during the spring of 1834, the Queen Regent named him Lieutenant Colonel of the cavalry forces under the command of Espinardo.

And this is the end of his military record. Nothing more. But his house and his board were always the haunt of brave officers. His most intimate friend, the Duke of San Carlos, was a soldier, whose charm was of the bluff sort. The two used to ride out together on beautiful thoroughbreds. People would turn in the street to look at them. Osuna frequently changed his horses, and he favoured the handsome Anglo-Arabians; the fringes and pompoms of their white silk halters shook as they arched their fine necks, curvetting and prancing on the promenade. Nobody sat a horse or drove a pair like Osuna. He and his friend San Carlos introduced this latter fashion in Madrid. With his throat swathed in black silk—the fashion of the day—or wearing a six-collared carrick Osuna promenaded his haughty languor in a gleaming carriage which he drove himself, avoiding with the greatest dexterity the confused cab-drivers and astonished pedestrians.

It was a long time before the tranquil phaetons grew accustomed to seeing a magnificent carriage driven by its owner while two expressionless flunkeys sat perched on the back. Listen to the biting, though not unkindly astonishment of the author of *Ayer, Hoy y Mañana:*

"The two young fellows in this carriage who sit there with arms crossed and without blinking an eye or moving a lip, are not being held up to the public gaze for any misdemeanour. It is no crime to be in service, and they are the servants of the coachman, who feeds them, clothes them, and pays them a good salary to drive them through the streets while one holds his cane and the other his snuff-box." And this is his bewildered comment at the sight of Osuna dashing by in his gig: "This other gentleman and this footman who rush by in a basket have not been forcibly thrust into it, nor is this a hamper, but the latest thing in rigs. It goes without saying that one of the riders, the coachman, is not just anybody, but a grandee of Spain; because today the better we are the commoner we try to appear."

IX. RUDDY SABLES

Je confondais l'odeur de la fourrure avec l'odeur de la femme.

BAUDELAIRE

THE animal dies but not its fur. Tanned and dressed, far from the blood which gave it life, the fur always preserves a warm caress for whomever comes within its gentle clasp. Furs have something feminine about them, like soft arms. For this reason Osuna was so fond of fur; the blood that coursed through his veins was blue and fleeting, and this man, so sensitive, so admired, and so lonely, sought shelter in his furs. He despised the world, and his feeble heart reached out toward a woman who would always be for him an inaccessible ideal, though Madrid does whisper that one night a tatter of cape was left on her balcony grille.

There you have him. This well set-up young man,

so dapper in his tight trousers and his snugly fitting boots of the best patent leather, has, if you look carefully, the bowed legs of all the gentlemen of his day. They were the last cavaliers, strictly speaking; men who afoot still kept the curve which riding or fencing had given to their muscles—*même quand l'oiseau marche . . .* —and they had the air of riders who have just jumped from the saddle, which makes it seem as though a horse were always an integral part of the picture.

But Osuna makes toward his conveyance, a carriage glittering with varnish; a splendid, high-spirited pair is hitched to it, impatient to be off, shaking the metal traces against the tongue, stamping their hoofs, and moving their tight-reined heads, with the little mirror in the middle of their forehead, blinders with silver crests beside their eyes, and stiff pompoms over their ears. Osuna's light foot releases the brake. The carriage turns. The horses prance. One footman hands his master the reins while another fastens around his shoulders a cape trimmed with bands of sable which like fair arms cling caressingly about his neck. The horses start off. There he goes like the wind. The day flees before him, like a living thing, restless, carrying everything with it, unattainable—for like Byron, the romantic lover can never believe that he has achieved the goal of his desperate yearnings.

Once in his palace, Osuna dresses for dinner. Today here, tomorrow there, he has only one day a week to gather at his table—"the Upper House" they call it—his friends and relatives "who acclaimed him the head of the family and of the caste," though he was barely twenty. He greeted his company with gay cordiality, reserving his sufferings for himself. D. Fernando Córdoba, who attended these dinners, gives the names and descriptions of the guests: the young Anglonas, cousins of the Duke; Antonio and Perico Santiago, known for their sharp, sarcastic tongue; the Duke of San Carlos, Navarrés, Casasola and his brother Cumbres Altas. At Osuna's right was the place of the respected and witty Count of Puñonrostro or of the Prince of Anglona, an uncle of the Duke "who was famous everywhere for his bad temper"; the veteran Eguía, the Count of Toreno, or the dashing Luis Fernández de Córdoba, celebrated for his military, gaming, and amorous exploits. There were also present Pinohermoso, Oñate, Parsent, and the deaf and imposing Duke of Frías "whose art consisted in concealing his vast wisdom."

The tone of these dinners, the jokes that spiced the conversation were, in keeping with the taste of the epoch, ingenuous, childish, or veiledly ribald, so as not to outrage the susceptibilities of these romantics who were ready to quarrel over straws, and risk life and fortune for a mere trifle. It was here that Don Luis Córdoba ventured to call the proud, crotchety Eguía "old," ". . . The King, whom you so cherish, expects everything from his *old* Eguía," he said amidst the hilarity of the noisy young folk gathered together there.

On occasion the jokes grew broader. "One night, over coffee and a certain Turkish liqueur which the Duke had supplied to him from Constantinople, when cigars had been lighted, and the servants dismissed, he called our attention to a mysterious painting which represented a beautiful, unknown woman, enveloped in furs which left only a glimpse of her divine countenance to view. All of us, old and young, were enchanted by the image which was the work of one of the leading artists in Paris; but my readers can imagine our surprise and emotion when, by touching a simple spring on the picture the clothing, furs and veils which hid the lady's secret charms began to disappear until she was finally in the same state as the two masterpieces of Titian in our National Museum. A salvo of applause followed, and Osuna received a magnificent ovation. "This"—Córdoba winds up—"will, I think, give an idea of the nature of these gatherings and of the Duke, in whom the serious and dignified representation of the first family of Spain, and his qualities as a brilliant public figure are not at all incompatible with a gay familiarity among his intimate friends."

Both the author and we are aware of the false and spectacular taste of a period that was dying away like the vibration in space of a note or a sigh.

The fashion of these pictures with a secret spring was not limited to that epoch. The famous mechanism by which one of Goya's *majas* covered up the other is well-known; the banker Salamanca was said to have a landscape in his country-place that covered a nude. A venial sin, if you like, but one in which the canker that was to corrode the epoch was manifest. Those palely pink, libidinous semi-nudes were devoured by the senile gaze of young men. In a trifling detail one sees a whole decrepit world whose capital sin is the worst and the most depressing: the sin of looking out of the tail of the eye.

X. D'ORSAY REIGNS IN EUROPE

Il faisait porter son medaillon jusqu'à des hommes.
BARBEY D'AUREVILLY

AND yet—despite his youth and splendour—Osuna was always a wan, tragic figure, steeped in melancholy. One night there was a great reception in the Neapolitan Embassy: the Prince and Princess of Partana received the élite of Madrid at a brilliant masked ball in their gilded salons. Everybody tried to outdo himself in luxury and splendour. The costumes of the men vied with one another in colour, appositeness, and richness. The ladies were dazzling with jewels and wore the most costly disguises.

The ball was well under way when, with languid, weary step, a masked figure appeared, behind whose domino a pair of murky eyes—the colour of dead turquoises—looked out. The face was the colour of ivory, the beard fair and full, the expression of the mouth scornful; the pleated white ruff, the black suit and tall hat were of the period of Philip II. This pallid shade was the Duke of Osuna, and the spectacle of his boredom and despair attracted the attention of the dancers:

Little blood in his veins
Deep night in his eyes.

These were the days when General Córdoba—an officer of the guards—while on duty fought four duels with four adversaries in a few hours, and Espronceda fought like a demon in a spur-of-the-moment duel alongside the walls of the cemetery of San Martin, under the awesome silence of the night, which held a cypress over its lips.

Beyond the Pyrenees the magnificent Count D'Orsay challenged an officer to a duel—the challenger stipulating that only the breast was to be exposed so that there would be no risk of disfiguring the face—for having blasphemed against the Virgin, and, consequently, offending a lady in his presence. It was incidents of this sort that gave D'Orsay such a vogue that the dandies of Europe imitated his gestures, his perfumes, his attitudes, and his neckcloths. One of these was Osuna, who after a sojourn in Paris brought back in addition to horses, carriages, paintings, and hats, an engraving of the Count. It was listed in his collections and from it he learned to tie his cravat in that immense black plastron which completely hid the throat. You can see him like this in the portrait which Madrazo did of him—only a few months before the Duke's death—his slender silhouette outlined by ruddy sables, against the luxuriant background of the patio of the Infantado palace in Guadalajara. He is to be seen in other effigies of these last years, dressed like D'Orsay: in oil paintings, miniatures and the famous bronze statuette made by Barré in Paris in 1839. Carlos Canigia had done a marble bust of him in Rome seven years before.

Don Pedro, who inherited from his grandmother the tendency to *se faire blanchir à Londres,* that is to say, of importing post-haste whatever new fashions were launched abroad, must have been one of the most unconditional admirers of that Alfred D'Orsay who conducted his trap, drawn by a horse caparisoned in a tigerskin, holding the reins on high, and displaying on his hand a lava ring, the gift of Byron who called him, the first time he saw him, "Cupid Unbound."

Brummel was Europe's captor but it was D'Orsay who seduced her with his charm. There are two methods of conquest, two styles, so to speak: by force, overcoming and subjugating, or by seduction, attracting and enamouring. Brummel was all daring impertinence, the fascination which dominates and is accepted because of the prestige it has acquired. D'Orsay was—by the testimony of his contemporaries—*le charme même,* which subjugates by the charm and fascination which emanates from it. It would not be far afield to suggest that, of the two Osunas, Don Pedro Alcantara was with respect to D'Orsay what his brother Mariano, later on, was to Beau Brummel. Different classes of dandyism due to analogies of temperament, barring, in each case, of course, the difference between the adventurer and the knight *sans peur et sans reproche.*

XI. SHE

Inés, alma de mi alma, perpetuo imán de mi vida.
ZORRILLA

THIS was Osuna: the fairy prince of the court. The gleam of his matchless fortune attracted the reigning beauties of his day; in short, the spoiled darling of all. And yet he did not marry. It was said that the object of his desires, the woman he loved, as love was then understood, belonged to another, and the impossibility of joining his life to hers constituted a torment which nourished his passion.

Respectful and gallant, he waited attendance on her everywhere; he danced with her at balls; he visited her at her palace, in her box at the opera, and he was to be seen, her assiduous escort, riding beside her gleaming blue carriage with its red bandings at the hour of the promenade on the Castellana.

Behold him, another Cupid, not unbound like D'Orsay. Enchained with jewels, pendants, fobs; about his throat the closely wrapped folds of his black neckcloth, his legs strapped and buckled, his breast criss-crossed with braided cords and decorations.

But she walked free, unhindered and untrammeled; one brusque shrug of her shoulders would have released her from her high-waisted grey dress, which left free two fair white arms. At times she wore a shoulder cape of silk, bordered with fur, and wore her hair parted down the middle, with golden corkscrew curls on each side of the face, and in the back a high jewelled comb around which the braid was coiled.

The very beautiful Doña Inés de Silva Téllez-Girón, Walstein and Pimentel was first cousin to Pedro, Duke of Osuna, daughter as she was of Don José de Silva, Marquis of Santa Cruz and of the famous Marchioness Doña Joaquina Téllez-Girón whom Goya painted reclining on a chaise longue, with a lyre in her hand and a chaplet of yellow leaves on her head. And this lovely marchioness, with her ingenuous, amazed eyes was in turn the daughter of Doña Maria Josefa, the Duchess of Benavente, and of her spouse the ninth Duke of Osuna.

Doña Inés first saw the light the twenty-first of January of 1806, the fourth daughter of this famous Santa Cruz cradle which had established a reputation as purveyor of beautiful women to the Spanish court. Doña Ines was not among the least favoured, and she soon became known as the most beautiful woman of her day, which, together with her marriage to the Marquis of Alcañices, Don Nicolas Osorio y Zayas—who laid at her feet seven grandeurs of Spain, a substantial fortune and the beautiful palace on Alcalá street, opposite the Prado—made her one of the leading figures among the aristocracy of her day. Here she shone until her death, which was caused by the epidemic of cholera which scourged Madrid the very year her son, the Duke of Sexto, was governor.

"The beauty of Madrid, par excellence," she was designated in the interesting memoirs of an anonymous diplomat who was at the court about the middle of the century. He says the marchioness was then in the neighbourhood of fifty. "As I did not know her when she was young, it is hard to imagine that she was ever more beautiful than now. Dark hair, like silk, ravishing eyes, teeth like pearls, exquisite hands and arms, all together enchanting," and he completes the description with a series of adjectives as effusive as they are vague; inasmuch as they can be used to define the most varied and even opposed types of beauty, provided they coincide in having silky hair, exquisite arms, teeth like pearls, ravishing eyes, and being altogether enchanting.

General Córdoba is not much more precise when he says: "The Marchioness of Alcañices is without rival at the court; her angelic face really seems that of one of Raphael's Madonnas."

But fortunately there are a number of portraits of her—in watercolours, oil, miniatures, marble busts—which bring us nearer to this elusive model.

Her face was pretty, with regular features, Cupid's bow eyebrows, a finely modelled nose with sensitive nostrils. It was delicately oval in shape and set upon a strong, matronly throat. Her expression was detached and romantic, without either fire or languish. A stolid, somewhat dull beauty. The most interesting thing about her is her look. She has almond-shaped eyes. Quiet, fixed, somewhat bovine, like those of her mother, like those of her son. Her expression is set, stamped like the printed flower on the cashmere shawl that trails from her shoulder; a cold, precise gaze that reflects the image with the same exact impassiveness as the convex mirror in the ebony frame that contrasts with the pink satin of her boudoir.

Her eyes are of the kind which—as it is generally phrased—have their gaze fixed on space. It is the look of those beings who pass serenely over the rope of life at its tensest, the look of a tight-rope walker. In their ecstatic gaze their seems to be reflected a background of horror. What do they see? What are they looking at when, in this strange way, they seem not to look? Are they seeking themselves there in space? Their gaze seems riveted on some definite and invisible point. Their whole unstable equilibrium depends upon it. Unless you want to make them fall, do not brusquely attract their attention. With arms out like a cross, a being lost in himself balances on the rope of eternity.

XII. RUSTLES IN THE ELM GROVE

Haute profusion de feuilles, trouble fier
Quand l'âpre tramontane
Sonne, au comble de l'or, l'azur du jeune hiver
Sur tes harpes, Platane.

P. VALÉRY

THE guests are on their way back to Madrid. The charabanc drawn by four grey thoroughbreds is already nearing Canillejas. The huge light beavers, the turbans and the flower-like sunshades which barely cover them are almost lost to view. The turn of the road has blotted out the cockade of the last footman perched up beside the umbrella-stock on the highest seat in the back. Osuna is left alone and pensative. The afternoon has been meaningless for him. Why all the merry-making and mirth? She was not there. Why? Did she not know that he was expecting her?

The afternoon has rolled by taciturnly in spite of

the agreeable company. All in vain did he drive the most beautiful of his guests through the grove in the charming little carriage drawn by four Shetland ponies which he uses inside the grounds. In the back perched two grooms in high hats, with high boots trimmed at the top with pink leather on their short legs. They drove down all the paths: through cypresses, elms, poplars, junipers. Wearied at last by the rattle of the little wheels beneath the varnished coach Osuna returns to the palace. He ascends the stairs beneath the condoling eye of the marble busts. He strolls about through the colonnades, under the medallions and the garlands which discreetly fold their stucco flowers because the master is not in a holiday mood. The sun goes down and the fountains cease their murmur. Osuna finds refuge in the library which Goya has decorated in an amiable, discursive, courtly mood.

Like his grandmother who built it, Don Pedro was passionately fond of the Alameda. There he hid his misanthropy during the summer months. There he expended great sums bringing an additional supply of water to ensure a luxurious vegetation, adding columns with fountains, busts and his coat-of-arms, and a fortress "à la Vauban," with cannon and a dummy gunner. He brought in broodmares and set up a racing stable of English thoroughbreds in the most approved British fashion, with jockeys, grooms, and trainers who were to bring triumph to the Osuna colours and put his monogram in the lead on the beribboned Jarretiera.

The first horse race in Spain, with gentleman riders, was held at the Alameda in the year '35. On April 23, 1841, Osuna, with his brother Terranova and friends like Veragua, Santiago, Perales, Santa Cruz, Casa Irujo, etc., founded the Society for the Improvement of Horse Breeding, of which he was the first president.

He added new attractions to the grove of the Alameda, that park dotted with *hameaux* and *bergeries* where the Versaillean tastes of the Duchess of Benavente were put to rout by a truculence typical of a Madrid street-fair, with swings and merry-go-round. The Alameda was not one of those absurd and adorable copies of a proper French garden. The romantic influence made it what is known, since then, as an English garden, and as such it is the only perfect model of its type in Spain, according to the gardening manuals of the day.

It has always pleased aristocrats to play like children, pretending to be shepherds, but after Rousseau this evil acquired grotesque proportions. The game was to return to nature without stepping outside the park. Later on the romantics would add dressed-up figures, rustic bridges, wooden cottages, ruined walls, surprises. That is to say, first they build a park in the heart of the country, and there they reconstruct an inoffensive, trained rusticity where their patent leather slippers and silk crinolines may pass undefiled. The beaux of the court dream of cabins and the idyllic existence of rustic lovers. The classic plan of the garden is beginning to lose its outlines: willows trail their branches over the lakes, and all sorts of amazing stage tricks are prepared for the edification of appreciative souls.

Other famous romantic gardens, like that of Osuna's in the Alameda, were laid out by the Count de Albon in Montmorency, by M. de Boulogne in La Chapelle, the Marquis de Giradin in Ermenonville, and so many others. And what ruins of fortresses and abbies were there, their delicate ogives muffled with ivy, jasmine and passion flowers. And at every turn a brooklet, a grove, a column, a sepulchre, a grotto, a cave, and, invariably, a little rustic wooden cottage painted to resemble an unpainted rustic wooden cottage.

The Alemeda and the Palace of the Infantado in Guadalajara

XIII. A TROUBADOUR'S ARIA

No lo oyes, de las auras al murmullo?
No lo pronuncia, en gemidor arrullo
la tórtola amorosa?
No resuena en los arboles que el viento
halaga con pausado movimiento
en esa selva hojosa?

GERTRUDIS G. DE AVELLANEDA

INÉS. There it is. The knife blade has bitten into the terse white skin of the sycamore, cutting a series of green lips from which oozes a little moisture. As the undefiled tree—*blanc comme un jeune Scythe*—exhales its grief it will murmur her name to the breezes. Don Pedro Alcántara has breathed it forth with his sighs wherever he goes. Inés, repeat the little birds of the Alameda in their twitterings.

In spite of the heat a restless desire drives him out along the paths, through the meadows. The dust there dulls the splendour of his patent leather; the well trimmed grass will bring it back. Fatigue possesses him as he goes along, tossing back his troubadour's mane, no longer worn in curls, but in loose ringlets. Back and forth, back and forth he goes; like every lover he tortures himself upon the rack, finding pleasure in his pain, flaying himself, like the tree: *l'impatient martyr—qui soi-même s'ecorche!*

Sunk in thought and oblivious to the natural beauties of his surroundings, Osuna keeps on. He crosses the greensward, breaks off a tender twig and reaches the bank of the lagoon. The ducks swim to meet him, trailing their submerged silhouette through the moiré of the water. But Don Pedro pursues his destiny without seeing them. Indifferently he passes before the tenderly grazing deer, and further on the brown camels, the hummocks of the desert, and the vain peacock who sweeps the park with his royal mantle.

The weeping willows droop their heads as he passes and offer him the fragrant caress of their green branches. It is a suffocating afternoon of late August, and solitary and restless, Don Pedro Alcántara has wandered on into the heart of the Alameda. It is not easy to recognize him without his high hat, his gold buttoned frock coat, his grey trousers and varnished boots. The heat and his profound misanthropy have led him to lay aside this attire, and he is simply dressed in vest and trousers of white linen, a coat of black alpaca, a low collar, and he carries in his hand a big *Bolivar,* one of those panama hats with large low crown and broad rolling brim, which look like a cross between a sailor and a silk hat.

He sits down for a moment in a little thicket. From his bosom he takes a locket with a miniature, and looking heavenward suddenly begins to sing. The rustle and murmurs in the foliage have ceased. Only the soothing voice of the fountain is heard among the leaves. The nightingales gather together; they interrogate one another in amazement, and each catches up in his beak a note which he carries off for his own trills and cadences.

The plaintive tumult has drowned out another, clearer and more incisive: that of the jubilant carriage which brought a lady out from Madrid with a joyous tinkle of harness bells (the tintinabullation of each bell is so persistent that it is like a dark spot which flees without ever finding the door).

The dusty wheels have drawn up before the palace —where they make a rut in the sand; the lathered horses paw impatiently. A hand taps for a moment at the lodge door and is withdrawn. A keeper in mutton-chop whiskers, duck uniform, bandolier, and breeches, stands in embarrassment, turning his hat round and round between his fingers.

"His grace is not in? Very good, then. Let's get back to Madrid."

He has given orders that he is in to nobody. She suspects that he has refused to see her. And by the time Osuna becomes aware of the sound of the harness-bells, the light chaise, with its yellow top raised against the dust and sun, is rapidly disappearing through the elms. A pair of handsome fiery black mares of the Alcañices breed give good account of themselves. So lightly, energetically, and sweepingly do they pace along that their movements resemble the complicated signature of the notary most adept at the caligraphic art.

As Osuna recognizes the sound of the bells in the air his song ceases; he sets out as fast as he can through the poplars, but he cannot overtake the carriage. Nevertheless he runs on. He rushes breathlessly through the deep sea of trees. His eyes seem about to burst from their sockets. He sees only green and blue pools overhead. He calls her; she will not hear him.

Don Pedro de Alcántara Téllez-Girón and Beaufort just before his Death

The lofty poplars flutter their hands despairingly to the sky. A heart-rending murmur still rustles through them.

Suddenly the trees grow larger, and the sky seems to draw away higher, further off. . . . Osuna feels the brusque contact of the earth against his knees. His legs no longer hold him up, everything is lost—woman, sky, life. . . . And he sinks into the depths of an overpowering swoon. Above, the leaves clamour incessantly; the sound of the bells grows more and more remote. . . . Stretched out in the poplar grove Osuna raves in his delirium. His sight is dim, he sees red, yellow. The swaying of near-by flowers seems to scatter a black dust into his eyes. . . .

What infernal power has maddened my brain?
Whence comes this horrendous vision?
This spirit . . . this black butterfly,
What is it? What would it with me?

He is borne post-haste to his Leganitos palace in Madrid, where he dies on August 25, 1844. Pedro Girón, the seventh of his name and the eleventh Duke of Osuna, was, according to the doctors' verdict, the victim of a cerebral hæmorrhage.

Five years later his remains, together with those of

his parents, were carried by his brother and heir, Duke Mariano, to the chapel of the Rest of the Holy Sepulchre in Osuna, where they received Christian and final burial. And there—shorn of his ruddy sables—lies Don Pedro Alcántara, the frustrated.

Part Three

MARIANO TÉLLEZ-GIRÓN

XIV. THE GOLDEN-HELMETED

The sharp goad that wounds the soul.
BECQUER

NIGHT dies as the day is born; one brother is extinguished that the other may live. Thus, the Dioscuri alternatively raise aloft their torches when the hour comes to substitute one another. At the moment of the change Jupiter says to the sacrificed Pollux: "If your love for your brother is so great that you wish to share his mortal destiny, half of your days must be spent in the shadows of the tomb, and the other half in the golden regions of the sky. . . . Thus Castor, the Golden-Helmeted, will behold the light again."

Now, in our story, Mariano, the second son, is the golden-helmeted. When the feeble torch of the older brother flickered out, there appeared in the night an impatient visage, crowned with fire and illuminated suddenly by ruddy gleams. Don Pedro Alcántara was the torch that was burning out; Don Mariano, a blazing brand.

Portraits of him as a child reveal a small, peaked face, a bright, secretive gaze, and over his forehead a flaming lock, a fiery saffron red. He brought with him haste, a delirium of grandeur, and a white-hot ambition, ready to forge unheard-of dreams. As a child, his torch was a fluted candle; then it became a sword of steel—and later, of flame.

Don Mariano Téllez-Girón and Beaufort was born, the second son of the tenth Duke of Osuna, in the very heart of Madrid on the nineteenth of July, 1814. Two days later he received the waters of baptism at the font in the parish church of San Pedro el Real near the Vistillas palace. In keeping with a custom much in vogue at the time, his godfather was a friar, the Reverend Father José Medrano, prior of the monastery of Santa Susana de la Trapa. A quiet, uneventful baptism.

The new Christian received the names of Mariano Francisco de Borja (for his illustrious forbear, the saintly Duke of Gandía) José Justo; and from that moment begins the lonely solitude which, in the last analysis, was the only companion of his life. That child, who was to inherit the greatest fortune in Spain, and totally consume it, to the greater glory and splendour of his name, had all his life long the intimate psychology of the disinherited, and perhaps this was why he fulfilled his destiny ruining himself.

Morally and physically Mariano's childhood was that of a neglected *poil de carotte* of a great family. He was a puny, unhealthy looking child whose frail shoulders supported a pathetic carroty thatch. His face was long, thin, and freckled; his mouth full and pursed in a disdainful expression; small, sharp, hidden little eyes; a high, prominent forehead crowned with unruly hair which gave him the look of a disagreeable little imp. All of him—and there was not much—had a proud, impertinent assertiveness, as of one who lives in constant fear of being passed by unnoticed. He was only a frail wisp of straw, but he was already on fire. He resembled Doña Josefa Pimentel in his unprepossessing looks and in his resentfulness.

The elder brother, who was intelligent and winning besides, had everything: for him the most flawless training befitting the heir to the throne. Mariano, the puny second son, received the off-scourings of this exquisite education. He, too, studied music, on the organ, and his lessons were heard by a dark, spectacled tutor who paid slight attention to his pupil. But neither the arts nor the humanities could find lodging in that vacant head, filled only with the smoke of its own fires. Outwardly, though, he suffered from cold. His feeble little fingers grew numb over the cracked oilcloth of the study table in a cold bare schoolroom; they passed without profit over the revolving sphere, the useless, corroded telescope, and as a last resort he put them in his mouth in quest of a little warmth. His childhood lacked sunshine; it could not ripen, and for this reason he always had a somewhat sour air.

The tenth duke, his father, Don Francisco de Borja Téllez-Girón, Pimentel and Pacheco, Marquis of Peñafiel, Count Ureña, etc., had been educated by the illustrious erudite Clemencín. For fervently espousing the cause of Fernando VII he was declared a traitor by King Joseph Bonaparte, and his rich possessions were confiscated; his brother Lieutenant General Don Pedro Alcántara, Prince of Anglona, Marquis of Javalquinto and head of the second branch of the family, was exiled for his liberal ideas.

Don Francisco de Borja Téllez-Girón, Tenth Duke of Osuna, father of Don Pedro

Mariano was not yet seven when his father—barely thirty-four—laid down once for all that fat round head, with its drooping lips and unhealthy complexion, which could barely support the locks of coarse lank hair. A few years later—January 28, 1830—his mother also passed away in the palace at Madrid: this flaccid, lymphatic flower of Flanders had never been able to acclimate herself. Heiress to the house of Beaufort and to its age-old vanity, she was a pompous, distant Juno who brought no warmth to her home. On her death she left her children rain-drenched possessions in Beauraing and a damp chill in their souls. The sole refuge of Don Mariano was the rigid guardianship of his grandmother, who took charge of him through his adolescence. This gave her time to stamp him with the haughty insolent acrimony which distinguished the Pimentels.

In feature the two resembled each other very much, barring the thanklessness of their respective ages. But what united them still more was this "psychic autointoxication" which corrodes, inflames, and sours the soul. It did not satisfy the Duchess of Benavente to be the lady of most elevated rank in Europe, cultured, intelligent, capricious, with a unique position, mistress of an immense fortune, whose sagacity and tart wit surrounded her with a court of admirers. There was something perpetually dissatisfied about her that pricked her on to seek abroad that which she could not find in her own country, and also perhaps to envy in others that which had been denied her: the charm and seductive beauty, for example, of her rival, the Duchess of Alba. The sound of her praises sung by poets and musicians, her court of wits, to whom her whim was law, was not enough to dispel the vexation aroused in her breast by the Duchess of Alba with her authentic court of lovers: Goya, the genius of the day, Cornel, *le vieux beau,* the gigolo Piñatelli, etc.

The Duchess of Benavente was inordinately despotic. She took it into her head to make an oasis in the desert, and in it *El Capricho,* a little Versailles. Time failed to abate her airs and her arrogance; she was given to curls, ribbons, bows, rosettes, feathers, flowers, brooches, laces, and gew-gaws of every sort. Seated amidst the pompous folds of her wide skirts of brocaded silk, little Mariano heard that cracked voice continually reminding him of his glorious ancestry—accompanied by the tinkle of collars, bracelets, pendants, and earrings of emerald and filigree—and inculcating in him a sense of the rights and prerogatives of a race whose motto in all its undertakings had always been: "Better to fly."

These chimeras were to take root in a mind whose natural impulses were weakened by a feeble constitution, and were to engender madness and delirium. For Mariano, power was a magnificent vision which he must keep ever present, but which fled from him, wooing the steps of the first-born.

I can imagine this child wandering about the Alameda, hiding his childish worries amidst those gloomy pavilions inhabited by the stuffed figures, and I see him change from timorous to rash. He has come to the parting of the ways. He must make a choice. A second son is nobody. As of old, there are only two paths open to him: the tonsure or the sword. A Girón does not hesitate. He must be a hero, with the desperate bravery of second sons who have nothing to lose. He will be a soldier, a cadet of the Guards. Besides, he has a strange plan, a secret mission that he unconsciously nurtures. His poor health, his sense of his position have kept him from being mischievous or disobedient as a child. "To be bad is to revenge oneself beforehand." He has not been, he never will be. His heart is encircled by a discipline as stiff as the triple collar of cloth, leather, and starched linen which makes up the halter of his Guard's uniform. And yet without his wishing or knowing it, behind that brooding, beetling forehead, a plot is being hatched against the omnipotent power of the head of the house. Later, when he himself clasps this sceptre which for the time being evades him, his hatred, enduring passionately, will shatter it to fragments.

XV. A SECOND SON'S EARLY DAYS

J'étais donc un dandy précoce.
BAUDELAIRE

WHEN the "sublime child," Victor Hugo, reached Madrid, his parents put him and his brother in school in the capital; and the thing that most attracted his attention was to see that no jot or tittle of ceremony was ever abated by the teachers when dealing with the young sprigs of Spanish aristocracy, going so far as to address them by all their titles and honours even when they were going to punish them: "My lord Marquis So-and-So, kindly get down on your knees and put on the dunce cap."

Typical son of Madrid though he was, Mariano never for a moment forgot that he was an Osuna. As a child he wandered alone and neglected amidst the treasures of tapestries and armour of the Vistillas palace. If he had only arrived first, he would have been all his fancy could have desired: Duke of Osuna. But life played him false at the first rendezvous. He would have to work hard to recuperate what had been lost. And he grows, and gets bigger, and holds his chest and head high, and curls his lips disdainfully, *closant les yeux a demi,* exactly in keeping with Barbey's formula for the dandy.

So far he is nothing but a "cockerel," trying to see how much he can spread his wings. And if we use the word "cockerel" it is because this was the term that was becoming popular for the young coxcombs who were just emerging from their shells. Mariano was one of them, and it was in his house that the word was first applied to a group of them. General Córdoba relates how he was presented by his brother to the famous Duchess of Benavente, Mariano's grandmother, who gave splendid receptions on Sundays for the cream of Madrid society, and how the Marquis of Santiago, "the most gallant figure of our day," was the one who first used the term, without suspecting, probably, that he was coining a new meaning which would pass into the Academy dictionary.

"One day a group of aristocratic young squirts were talking together in one of the drawing-rooms of the palace on the Cuesta de la Vega, and they were making such an uproar, an inveterate habit in Spanish gatherings, that Santiago, who was near by, shouted out: "Not so much noise from the cockerels."

The term found favour and everybody used it. The author of *Ayer, hoy y mañana,* says *à propos* of it: "After the table is cleared the fencing foils are taken down, for these are an indispensable decoration on the walls of a cockerel's room, and they give and parry a few thrusts."

There is another version of the term's origin, according to which a lady, on being importuned by a young man who was loath to take no for an answer, said to him: "It is because you are too much of a cockerel."

Be its origin what it may, the expression came into being and popularity because the impotent, overbearing atmosphere of the period required it. These are the words of a contemporary, Mesonero Romanos: "I realized then that I was a cockerel, and that I was entering upon a world whose gullibility, futility, and callowness put it on my own level."

XVI. DISDAIN WITH DISDAIN

Je n'ai vu dans le monde que des diners sans digestions, des soupers sans plaisirs, des conversations sans confiance, des liaisons sans amitié, et des coucheries sans amour.
CHAMFORT

ITS own exuberance has worn it out, and cracks are beginning to appear on the surface of romantic idealism. The flowing, unbound curls are becoming lank uncombed locks which catch the dust of an epoch that is falling into ruin. The nineteenth century is moving forward like a broken-down wagon, creaking over dusty rubbish piles. In the drawing-room, frills and starched collars, courtly gestures and studied manners are still in use. But polite impertinence is obliged to step haughtily aside for bold insolence. The noblest and most proper gentlemen laugh at jokes that are decidedly reprehensible. It is the vulgarity of a decaying age, which is taking complete possession of it.

So witty and well-bred a person as Fernando Córdoba caused a terrible hurly-burly once as a religious procession was going by because he was ordered to take off his hat in a way he did not like. The cream of Madrid society went to visit him while he was under arrest and talked about nothing else. And he himself relates, as an example of a "youthful prank," an anecdote of the noble Marquis of Santiago, which may be cited as typical:

Scene: the palace of the Duchess of Benavente at the Puerta de la Vega, which society called the "Ottoman Gate." Characters: the ever-beautiful Marchioness of Alcañices; a blue-blooded English lord who had just presented his credentials as British Ambassador, and the Marquis of Santiago. There are other secondary figures: Don Pedro Osuna, who intervenes at the crucial moment, lovely Encarnación Camarasa—Don Pedro's cousin and sweetheart—who was singing at the piano; the Duchess on her dais; ladies, famous artists, gentlemen in evening clothes, officers of the Guard, etc. The Englishman asks to be presented to the ladies. He is introduced to the Marchioness of Alcañices just as some "musical selections" are being given, and he wants to ask her if she is fond of music. He takes Santiago to one side and asks him to dictate a polite phrase in Spanish to him. Santiago does so and the Englishman, with the words fresh in his ears, goes straight to the Marchioness and blurts out: "Madam, you are a big stork."

Anger of the lady. Consternation of the lord. Laughter and comments of the spectators. Madrid society chuckles over it as another stunt of Santiago, the playboy. But the diplomat could not see it in the same light. It seemed to him that the Marquis had a perverted sense of humour, and he sent his seconds to visit him. Santiago named D. Pedro Alcántara, in whose house the incident had taken place. Osuna employed all his tact and urbanity, and "it was with great difficulty that he was able to bring to a satisfactory end an affair which had afforded the *haute monde* of Madrid much food for gossip and laughter."

There was one who contemplated all this with an outwardly interested and eager air, but at heart he was profoundly disdainful and disillusioned. The curl of his lip was becoming more scornful; his eyelids drooped still lower. It was as though he were approaching the throne of all this splendour with an infernal machine under his cloak. He smiled and let things take their course. When his turn came, there would be an end to all this. He would leave no more trace of his own palace than his ancestor the Count of Benavente had left of his in Toledo after the perfidious duke had defiled it with his presence.

As a first step he would have to exile himself from this unhealthy, suffocating atmosphere. Gone were the days when a Téllez-Girón would have been a colonel at the age of ten; he would have to begin as a soldier. And so, spurning a world which did not appreciate him, he cut himself loose from the moorings of his house; at the age of nineteen he embarked on his military career as cadet of the Royal Guards. This same year his brother ceded to him the marquisate of the city of Terranova in Italy, with the rich possessions pertaining to it.

When his grandmother, Doña Maria Josefa Pimentel, saw him thus provided for and prepared to buffet the storms of life, she gave way—perhaps for the first time in her existence, and out of deference to her adversary—before Death, and on the fifth of October, 1833, in her palace on the Cuesta de la Vega, departed this world at the ripe age of eighty-two.

XVII. THE PRODIGAL SON

J'ai un esprit vengeur de torts et fort inclin a la justice distributive.

C. DE BERGERAC

On February 27, 1833, Don Mariano Téllez-Girón, Marquis of Terranova, was appointed supernumerary cadet of the second brigade of the first squadron of the Royal Bodyguard. On July 14 he was put on the payroll and passed into active service. And one of his first assignments was on October 3 of that same year.

It was early in the morning, and over the bridge of San Fernando passed an endless chain of carriages and riders, escorting a funeral coach, drawn by six mules caparisoned in funereal draperies, which was conducting the body of Fernando VII to the Escurial. They travelled the entire day. On the barren height of Galapagar it suddenly grew dark. The lights of the funeral train flickered, blown about by the cold winds. The corpse had to be laid in the church for the night.

At dawn the procession resumed its march. Scudding clouds flitted across the sky. The retinue struggled on in silence to reach the monastery becalmed on its granite sea. When they reached the church, a series of transfers began: from the warden to the abbot, from the abbot to the gentlemen of the bedchamber, from the gentlemen of the bedchamber to the Order. . . . And all these negotiations of responsibility amidst clouds of incense, prayers, holy water, and chants which reverberated through the chill vaulted temple dome. And once more, summons, delivery and identification, as though there were someone who wished to steal the body. Then the descent to the crypt with feebly gleaming torches, while scabbard tips clank against the stone steps. A few paces further. A halt. "Mind the step." Wax that drips on tricornes. More sprinkling with the hyssop. More requiems. As the coffin is lowered one of the marble steps cracks. It seems to Mariano Terranova in this gloomy dungeon that he has left the world behind. Like his king, he is entering on another existence. He is attending his first funeral.

Back in his palace once more, he finds the old familiar warmth and friends. Yet even here his position is not assured. His brother at the head of the table gathers about himself the "Upper House"—restraint, poise, assurance. Mariano goes with the younger group: Cimera, Gayoso, etc., who make up the "Lower House"—youth, impatience, revolt. At the hour of the liqueurs the older ones, less prodigal of themselves, smoke and talk in the drawing-room, while Mariano, with other officers of the Guard, goes about from gathering to gathering, as was the custom of the day. At some they find words of encouragement from the lips of their veteran battle-scarred hosts, Ahumada, Ezpeleta, Puñonrostro, who were gallant generals in their day. But none had greater enthusiasm for the profession of arms than the lovely Marchioness of Santa Cruz, who made much of her nephew Terranova and the other cadets who visited her palace, telling them that to her way of thinking there was no career so gallant, nor could she understand "how a gentleman could select any other."

Afterwards the officers went to the theatre, where they sat apart from the civilian public; or gambled at ecarté or monte. The sky was the limit for Mariano Terranova at this pastime, and the money slipped through his fingers like water. The plentiful income from his holdings was not enough to take care of his horse, and it was common knowledge that his brother had to provide for all his expenses.

But rising hours were early; companies had to be ready for review in the Prado at dawn. As the honour squadron passed it saluted the stern-visaged Count of Spain with its swords.

A few hours later, in the same place and with the same uniforms, it saluted the ladies. For in those days, "uniforms were not reserved exclusively for military purposes, but their bright colours, gold braid and trimmings were by preference displayed among the groups of lovely ladies." In their desire to behold beauty at closer range, even at the risk of being trampled by the horses, Córdoba, the Conchas, and other officers of the Guard introduced the custom of strolling along the side of the road. After them, Mariano Terranova, Zabala, Pezuela, La Bastida, and so many others would promenade in their tight-waisted uniforms and their high red collars alongside the carriages.

Under no consideration would they wear civilian

clothes. At the Palace in the evening, or at dances or receptions they appeared in full-dress uniform, gold-braided tricorne, buckled slippers, silk hose, and knee breeches. It is even said that the latter garment gave rise to whispers and smiles among the ladies, for not all the officers of the Guard had calves as shapely as those of Muñoz, which had helped him ascend the steps of the throne.

The youthful Marquis of Terranova attended these dances at the royal palace, or at those of Partana or Fernán-Nuñez, picking his way carefully over the waxed floors to avoid stepping on a train or catching his spurs in a ruffle, with one arm folded over his heart, holding his tricorne: *C'est la foule, on est seule on ces salons dorés, le bal joyeux nous cache aux regards effarés,* wrote Victor Hugo about this time.

Mariano Terranova performed the prescribed rites and ceremonies, and little by little he began to feel that peculiar suffocation produced by lights, the rustle of silks, women's backs, smoothly fitting bodices, laughter, satin, the glitter of jewels—all taking him by the throat, which, to make matters worse, was swathed in that choking red collar. In that warm light —which like the music pervaded all, intimately blending one thing with another—he too felt kindled and animated and on the verge of melting away like those huge candles which shone from the enormous chandeliers which were replenished at the dinner hour. The substitution was made by a squad of servants, each with his ladder, who appeared in the momentarily deserted drawing-rooms, like scene shifters on the stage. Meanwhile the guests quenched their thirst in the dining-room for a few moments.

All the following year of 1834 Terranova was on duty with the Guards during the Royal visits to La Granja, Riofrio, and El Pardo. The next year he was in Segovia until the middle of September. The amusement of his salad days were the jaunts through the forest, the gay repartee with the ladies in the low-ceilinged drawing-rooms, which one reached through a corridor covered by lithographs, and flanked by stiff rows of rush-bottomed chairs, and the nocturnal trysts with handmaidens of one kind or another. But, in spite of everything, the life of an officer on duty was a monotonous existence, and in the distance he could hear the clamour of war. Meanwhile this prodigal son was spending huge sums on gambling and adventures, following the caprices of a weak will, that is to say, wilful. Don Mariano was already "the prodigal from lack of will power," as Silvela diagnosed him years later when of his past splendour there remained only some forty million pesetas in debts.

Then suddenly, with a proud, scornful gesture, Mariano Terranova leaves for the war. In the North the cannon were roaring. In Madrid a group of young intellectuals, known as the Thunder Party was firing broadsides of facetiousness at the bourgeoisie. And a radiantly beautiful, bejewelled woman had arrived mysteriously from Brazil and had taken society by storm with her talent and her originality. Maria Bushental brought to Madrid the first sparks of the modern spirit.

XVIII. NOBLESSE OBLIGE

The Duke prefers to be called General and have a Colonel as his aide rather than be called Duke and have a First Secretary of the Legation for his secretary.

JUAN VALERA

TRUE knight that he was, Don Mariano Girón could scent combat from afar. Like all his race, he found on the battlefield his real calling and vocation, "beyond doubt the best and most honourable today," he himself was to write the next year on the eve of the bloody struggles which were to win him the cross of St. Ferdinand.

Twenty years later Juan Valera will describe how the Duke wore his uniform all during the trip to Russia, how he endured temperatures of 14° below zero while reviewing troops, and preferred the title of General to any other. One of the bright phrases coined by Madrid was that "there was a Duke (Osuna) who liked to be called General, and a General (Serrano) who liked to be called Duke." In truth, a dismounted noble gives the impression of having been thrown from his saddle; a knight is perforce a centaur. And once mounted, he needs his arms—titles and honours are for courtiers.

At last we have Terranova sword in hand; his horse is champing at the bit. It is the month of September of 1835 and on the twenty-first he leaves with his fourth squadron to join the army of the North under Brigadier-General Restán's command. Here he serves his first apprenticeship, receives his baptism of fire, and then receives a Royal Order to return to Madrid to join the staff of General Palafox, Duke of Zaragoza, who has just been made Captain-General of Aragon.

Don Mariano Téllez-Girón never accepted a salary. He had donated the remuneration due him as a cadet to the corps infirmary, and this trait lasted all his life. He never accepted the travelling expenses, perquisites, and pensions due him, which would have amounted to large sums, especially toward the close of his ruin. Among the many who profited by the millions he squandered, his country stands at the head.

The commander-in-chief of the supporters of the Queen Regent at the time was the gallant Don Luis Fernández de Córdoba, who fired the soldiers and the nation with the passion he put into his command. He was inspired by a lofty ideal and he was impulsive and generous. The most select of the officers were anxious to be at his side and follow his standard. Mariano Terranova, who had always been his admirer, was able to prove how firm and loyal was his adhesion, which remained unshaken during the trying days to come for Córdoba.

By a Royal Order dated December 27, 1835, Osuna was made aide-de-camp to the General in command, and, as Cadet of the Guards, Captain of the cavalry forces. He received his appointment in January. He made his preparations quickly and contentedly, and in February of 1836 he presented himself before General Córdoba in Logroño, with the best horse, the most impeccable uniforms, the richest equipment and the most ardent spirit ever exhibited by a cadet in the sanguinary campaigns of the North.

The winter of 1836 was a bitter one on the field; "the snow lay two and three yards deep." When General Headquarters were transferred to Vitoria "the fog was so heavy" that operations were continually in danger of surprise attacks and ambushes. But that turbulent crowd of young officers who were seeking the outlet for their energies which later generations would find in sports, was reluctant to resign itself to a winter of inactivity in Vitoria. Some gambled and flirted; others improvised dances and music: "the sound of a wheezy piano or an untuned guitar often mingled with the roar of the cannon." At Córdoba's headquarters, besides his brother Fernando and Terranova, there was the latter's cousin, Javalquinto, of the Anglona family; three of Puñonrostro's sons; the youthful and cultivated Count of Campo Alange, a writer who was nipped in the bud; another incipient author, Ros de Olano; a coming hero, José de la Concha; Escosura, who was witty as well as brave; Moriones, Malibrán, etc. . . . all of whom were more interested in adventure and excitement than promotion.

Combats with the enemy failing, they never lacked for bickerings among themselves, and an occasional serious episode with swords or pistols. At other times they joined the troops that were going out to forage, in the hope of a skirmish. Córdoba describes, as a common occurrence, something that reads like a polo match, with prisoners as trophies, instead of cups. They were in the habit of riding out on horseback, accompanied by their orderlies, to a broad meadow where they would practise running, jumping, taking walls, hedges, ditches, and other natural obstacles. Both horses and riders acquired dexterity. One day, on their way back, they met an enemy squad in the road. They charged them with riding crops as they were not carrying arms and managed to knock three Carlists out of the saddle. It was growing dark, as the group of officers rode carelessly into Vitoria, smoking and talking as they went. Amidst the shadows of the evening and the tired feet of the horses skulked the prisoners they had taken.

And every day things like this. Fernando Córdoba tells about another unpremeditated exploit, which cost his faithful Curpín's life, and in which Mariano Terranova took part. Córdoba had volunteered to do some reconnoitring, accompanied only by Curpín and some soldiers of Navarre, who had deserted from the Carlists, for in his opinion "the Navarrese are the best soldiers in the world when they make common cause with their officers; they fight to the last ditch, they conquer without cruelty . . . and provided they have wine and a guitar, they would rather dance than sleep."

He picked out his men and they saddled their horses. "My brother-officer, Don Mariano Téllez-Girón, now Duke of Osuna, wanted to come with me and bring along his cousin Don Pedro, the Marquis of Javalquinto. When the time came we set out and in a little while we had a skirmish on the banks of the Zadorra."

Spurred on by their triumph they pushed further and further ahead, in the direction of Villarreal, till they discovered a squadron of the enemy. They drew nearer, observed them and "being close by it seemed to me that it would be an easy matter to fall on them, stir up a commotion, execute a brilliant manœuvre, give Javalquinto his initiation, and win for us all the cross of St. Ferdinand. No sooner said than done. We set off at a gallop and then we charged them, hurling ourselves blindly upon them. But as they scattered they revealed a company of infantry hidden among the rocks which received us with a hail of bullets." He goes on to tell of the surprise, the confusion, the fight, the rescue of the wounded, with Mariano Osuna and the orderlies defending their rear, and causing losses among the enemy, of Curpín's mortal wound, Córdoba's grief, and this final commentary, after the escapade: "Javalquinto conducted himself with distinction in his first feat of arms. The Duke of Osuna behaved like a veteran." What he longed for were these crosses of St. Ferdinand—soon to be his—and for them he exposed his breast to the sword's point.

XIX. LONG LIVE THE QUEEN

THIS was war, and now "good or bad 'tis but the chance of war," as in *Troilus and Cressida.*

"Adjutant Girón," called the commanding General, "give the lines the order to fire."

And instantly Mariano Terranova galloped past the outposts, tricorne in hand, to the cry of "Long live the Queen!", a shout which warmed the cockles of the brave general's heart. The first reports rang through the air, and the fiery forelock of the adjutant was lost from sight as it sped ahead, and the firing from the trenches began.

Another time it is some delicate commission or a bit of stealthy reconnoitring where the horse must be left tied to a tree a good distance off so the enemy will not hear it. Terranova performed a number of services of this sort, took part in the assault and bombardment of the castle of Guevara on the sixth of April, and again a few days later in the action at Miñano Mayor, against the Carlist berets Villarreal commanded.

A post on the staff of a grandson of the Grand Captain was far from being a mere curvetting about on horse-back or preening for reviews or dress parades. He demanded a great deal from his splendid staff, this gallant Fernández de Córdoba, because he gave a great deal. The general had great projects on foot, and Mariano Terranova had no time to rest. May was ushered in with a number of different operations against the town of Murguía and the valley of Lodosa. Terranova took part in all of them, as well as in the reconnoitre of the castle of Guevara on the second. The troops in the castle thought it was a regular attack and opened heavy fire, but it was only a bit of strategy, and the Liberal troops kept on their forward march. The division Don Mariano was with captured positions in Arlabán and Adana, and flanking the main body of the army which was marching on San Adrián, came out at Galarreta. They fell upon the vanguard with such force that they made themselves masters of those sierras, climbing over cliffs, briars, and rocks to a rough little upland where to their astonishment they found a small shrine amidst the thickets. It belonged to Our

Lady of Aranzazu, which in Castilian means: "You among the thorns?"

The hotspurred Terranova was never to forget this brush. It was the twenty-second of May and Córdoba was already in the thick of the battle of San Adrián, where his soldiers climbed "higher than the snows of May, and saw the eagles flying beneath their feet," as he put it in his ringing proclamation. He was effectively supported by generals like Espartero, Rivero, and Oráa, who at this very battle, when he received the news of his son's death, exclaimed: "Tell the Queen I'm sorry I have no more sons to serve her."

The morning of the twenty-third Mariano Terranova was honourably mentioned for bravery in action, and received special thanks in Her Majesty's name. He also received an abundant ration of meat and of good Rioja wine out of the booty with which the General's staff regaled the aides-de camp, as Fernando Córdoba recalled in later years. And Terranova managed, that same day, to have a share in the fighting at Salinas de Guipuzcoa.

There was time for everything except rest. Attacks followed one another like reports from a machine gun. On the next day, when the troops were camped on the heights of Arlabán, the Carlists suddenly tried to retake the positions. It was a hard struggle and the battle lasted all day. On the twenty-fifth the army massed at Villarreal and under a hail of enemy grenades they wiped out the Carlist defences. But the next day the army went into billets.

May was not yet over when Madrid was surprised by the arrival of the Commander-in-Chief and his favourite adjutants, Terranova, Casasola, Javalquinto, and Fernando Córdoba. Public opinion was divided about the campaign and Luis Córdoba presented himself of his own accord at court to render his accounts with the haughtiness traditional in his family under such circumstances.

He was received with great interest by all, and with cheers and applause on the part of some. But Mendizabal was a hard enemy. Why had the campaign not been finished? There were a number of ministerial councils, and at the end of June a famous one at the Pardo. The two Córdobas and Terranova sat at the table with the Queen, and Her Majesty did her best to transmit the enthusiasm of her faith and confidence to all. But the gentle eyes of the Queen Regent were sadder and more wistful than ever that day. When the session was over a carriage galloped back toward Madrid at breakneck pace. Inside, taciturn and gloomy, rode the two Córdobas and Terranova. On the box sat Discouragement, holding the slack reins.

Back in the North once more they followed the orders they received from the War Office. But Terranova's proud blood boiled at this affront to his friend and general, and in the first engagement he demonstrated his bravery. It was on July 4, in the battle of Zubiri, on the banks of the Iñigo and Gurruchaga. In "that long, hard-fought struggle, for which Villarreal had massed all his forces, the enemy was driven back at every point" by General Córdoba. The cavalry of the Guards "made a brilliant charge, fighting hand to hand with the Carlist infantry, and taking over two hundred prisoners. Don Mariano Téllez-Girón distinguished himself in this action, and for the valour he displayed he was decorated on the battle-field with the cross of St. Ferdinand of the first order."

During the month of July also Girón took part in the operations at Peñacerrada. August found him engaged in the pursuit of General Gómez, and on various movements through the valley of Mena and in Orduna.

But the solidarity of the army was broken, and Mariano, moving from place to place, lonely and discouraged, felt himself once more a puppet, a spectre, a glittering, hag-ridden shadow.

XX. THE SCARLET CROSS

As his only Spanish insignia
The cross of Calatrava.

DUKE OF RIVAS

THE general staff had been dispersed. Separated from his general, Mariano Terranova was out of active service in Vitoria during the month of October, 1836, but not idle. He was looking for a man he could becomingly serve. He felt drawn to General Oráa, whose heroic mettle had been revealed not long before at San Adrián. A Girón cannot deign to serve a leader he does not admire. This kept him undecided and vacillating. His friends, Pezuela, Urbina, etc., began to worry. Some suspected a change of ideas or party. They also thought that perhaps this capricious man—now that he had won the cross of St. Ferdinand—would lack the stamina to continue in his enthusiasms. Wilful and changeable, it was essential for him to aspire to something he had not yet attained. One of his more faithful friends, Campo Alange, encouraged and stood by him: "Oráa is favourably inclined toward you," he wrote him, "and is willing to make a place for you."

Mariano Osuna was always a lonely soul. He was an ideal friend, loyal, generous, but loath to yield to a real intimacy. But Don José de Negrete, Count of Campo Alange, was really his friend, "perhaps the only one," Don Mariano wrote him on the twenty-eighth. And now he proved it by securing him a post in Oráa's retinue, together with himself and La Bastida.

Mariano's enthusiasm revived, and he expressed his gratitude to Campo Alange in terms that are not only sincere but touching. Not a trace of misanthropy is left in him. He began to make his preparations. He looked for a horse, as he had sold his mare to Urbina and had no mount; he wanted to join the troop at once. But at this very juncture the impetuous Count of Campo Alange, as scant in years as rich in military and literary promise, received a mortal wound in the siege of Bilbao. And now what? Mariano asked himself. Where can this taciturn, riven Girón turn?

Once more he hesitated, fluctuated. As a result of the events in La Granja his associates had been scattered. Luis Córdoba was in France. Fernando, Abadía, the Puñonrostros, in Madrid. Terranova remained with Espartero, Commander-in-Chief in the North at that time. As his aide-de-camp, and afterwards with Alaiz, who was in command of the Third Division, he took part in all the operations that year. Those were grey, monotonous days, shrouded in the foggy drizzle of the North. Suddenly there came a clearing, a red streak in the grey: on November 27, 1836, Her Majesty bestowed on him the habit of Calatrava. When his patents of nobility were established the following July, Don Mariano—first going through a novitiate—was made a knight of the illustrious order, whose emblem, which his race had always reverenced, he always wore, as well as the cape, which he liked to wear over his richest and most elaborate uniforms: a white sail, beside which the very snow seemed jaundiced, with which, when Duke of Osuna, he launched himself on the perils and fortune of the frozen seas of All the Russias.

At the sign of this red brand Girón felt his bellicose ardour resurge, just as the war was flaring up again, and with greater violence. It was brave Espartero who led the troops and Mariano Terranova sought permission to join him in his hazards. Early in 1837 he left for Bilbao, where he joined the staff of Count Luchana, and took part in the operations at Zornoza, Durango, and Elorrio.

It was in the month of May when Espartero got ready to advance against the fortified sector of Hernani, after making his preliminary surveys around San Sebastian. The hopes of all Spain, and England who was allied with her, were pinned on the bravery and daring of this leader. The story runs that at a banquet which Lacy Evans gave for Espartero and his staff, the general proposed a toast to the first grenadier to enter Hernani. To which Seaone added the offer of a pension for the hero, whereupon Carondelet remarked that they had better exclude the Commander-in-Chief from the competition, because he might forget the obligations of his rank and snatch the glory from a private soldier.

In the reconnoissances carried out on the eleventh and twelfth, Terranova could appreciate the strength of the apparently impregnable positions of the Carlists along the banks of the Urumea and on the heights of

Oriamendi. Espartero's troops, which were camped in the flats where they were exposed to the full fury of the violent storms that were raging those days, began to move slowly on the sixteenth, advancing through Oyarzun. Soaked with mud and rain they reached the fortifications of Irun, which put up a tenacious resistance. The artillery was found to be useless, so the soldiers had to hack their way through. After a thirty-six hour siege, Irun capitulated. In this fierce attack Don Mariano Téllez-Girón won another cross of St. Ferdinand of the first order.

They moved ahead and on the eighteenth the firing was so heavy that their ammunitions gave out in the capture of Fuenterrabia. Espartero, and with him his aide-de-camp, were after a complete victory, and gave the army no rest, nor took into account the heavy losses on both sides. Don Mariano distinguished himself in the action at Urnieta, on the parapets of Andoain, on the twenty-ninth; at the capture of Santa Cruz de Arezo, the thirty-first, and on June first at Lecumberri, where once again he received: "Special Honourable Mention and Her Majesty's personal thanks."

On the second he took part in the fighting between Urquiz and Berrioplano, and he continued like this until later in the month he was sent with the general staff of the expeditionary forces to Aragón, against the army headed by Don Carlos, and he served through this campaign and that of Cuenca.

From Torrelaguna he was sent to Madrid on matters connected with the service. He happened to be there on the morning of September 12th, when he was struck by something strange in the atmosphere of the capital. The Reserves were massing in the side streets; people, pale with fear, were rushing to take refuge in their homes. Panic had seized the population at the unexpected news that the Carlists were about to enter the city. Terranova had his horse saddled with all speed. At that very moment Fernando Córdoba had done the same thing, and when he appeared before the Captain-General of Madrid to offer him his services, the latter answered in utter despair: "Today the Carlists will be in Madrid."

But Córdoba fearlessly rode to the Prado. There he assembled all the soldiers he could, and a group of "officers of the Guard, experienced and brave," to use his own words, and they went out by the walls of the Retiro, ready to die fighting off the attacks of Cabrera, who, with a great army, had taken the Liberals by surprise, and was marching on the capital. Córdoba wanted to attack, but was dissuaded. Then, with Terranova, he made a reconnoissance near Vallecas, spreading out his meagre cavalry forces fanwise. This sufficed to halt the enemy who perhaps thought this was the vanguard of a large army. Afterwards other reasons made withdrawal advisable; but the first attack was staved off by the bravery of the officers of the guard.

Terranova still participated in the operations that followed until the Pretender took refuge in the Northern provinces. But he was in poor health. He was only twenty-three, and his breast was covered with crosses like Mt. Calvary. He had reason to be proud; nevertheless, he was dissatisfied. During two years of hard campaigning he had fought like a Trojan. He had been worthy of his name. On his return to the court the women—who for a moment had feared that they would fall into Cabrera's tiger claws—looked upon him as a hero. His family was uneasy about his health. They obliged him to obtain a royal leave of absence in December to recuperate. And in January he crossed the frontier, like the other leaders and officers of the Liberal army, to France. Little is known of him there.

As a matter of fact, little is ever known of anybody at this age, when all that is not action is still a mystery. Mariano Osuna was unknown and he was himself his only companion.

XXI. IN THE DANDIES' NATIVE HAUNTS

Rien ne reussissait à Londres comme l'insolence.
A. DE CHATEAUBRIAND

IN retiring from active military service and at the same time expatriating himself, Don Mariano Osuna achieved a supreme act of foppishness. He felt the "ungrateful fatherland" like the romantic dandy, and the imperious urge to absent himself for ever, and, as a matter of fact, from then on he spent the greater part of his life outside of Spain. For the time being, neither his delicate health nor the attitude of Espartero toward Córdoba and his friends made it possible for him to return to the battlefield.

On January 16, 1838, her Majesty made him reserve officer of the Royal Guards, and shortly afterward he was appointed military attaché to the Embassy

Extraordinary sent to London for Queen Victoria's coronation.

He went to London via Paris, and he met there no small number of Spanish emigrés, especially in a hotel in Regent street, where they foregathered. He made the trip to Calais in one of the Lafitte stagecoaches. Trains were still few and left much to be desired. The élite of English society travelled only by stagecoach or post and avoided railroads, not so much because of fear of losing their lives in an accident as of getting their delicate-hued trousers or frock-coats smudged with soot or smoke.

To be sure, Beau Brummel was already carefully rubbing all hints of newness from his raiment, and British society was entering upon the grey, stolid, middle-class, comfortable Victorian doldrums . . . but the Count D'Orsay took the gates in Hyde Park on horse-back, and the one strident note in the symphony of Victorian complacency was that of the dandies.

The dandy's motto is well-known: "Stay where you are until you have made your effect, and as soon as you have produced it, leave." And this device was belligerently hoisted by *lyons* and *macaronis*, *beaux* and *currutacos, fashionables* and *petimetres, gants-jaunes* and *cocodés, boquirrubios* and *pisaverdes*—by all these names they were known—wherever they went, and all their acts were guided by a spinose Muse: Impertinence—the daughter, according to Barbey, of Self-assurance and Frivolity, and the sister of Wit.

The Victorian court was so dowdy that it made the English blush. Charlotte Brontë opined of the Queen, when she saw her go by, that she was a nice woman, but without a particle of distinction. Of the Prince-Consort the aristocrats said: "He's a perfect gentleman, but what impossible frock-coats!" The English beau, logically enough, responded to this lack of fastidiousness by exaggerating his refinements, and opposing a dazzling elaborateness to the dull constraint of the court. "He must have," writes Chateaubriand in 1839, "an air of superiority, insouciant, insolent; he must take great pains with his toilette, wear his beard or moustache carefully trimmed . . ." and he contrasts him with the romantic young man of fashion of 1822 who: "cultivated a suffering, unhealthy appearance, carelessness of dress, a beard neither full-grown nor trimmed, as though it had come upon him by surprise in an hour of distraction when racked by his torments, a lock of hair fluttering in the breezes; a profound, exalted, detached, unearthly expression in his eyes; his lips curled by scorn for humanity at large." He seems to be drawing the portrait of Don Pedro Alcántara de Osuna, the Frustrated.

Don Mariano followed the fashions of his day to the letter, and always looked as though he had just stepped out of a band-box, with his moustaches waxed to a point and a haughty, impertinent air.

The purpose blindly assigned him by his epoch is to triumph, and triumph he would, let it cost what it would.

It was not necessary for him to make an effort to attract attention by *faire le fat,* as Stendhal suggests, disguising his true self. He was naturally fatuous. Vapid, pompous, unsubstantial, his was the vacuity of the ephemeral soap bubble; his own iridescence and amazing contour dazzled him. It was possible for the dandy to be a fool and yet arouse interest. *Barbey d'Aurevilly, formidable imbecile,* says Victor Hugo. Hazlitt called Byron a sublime fop, who in turn called

Wordsworth "an idiot in his glory." There is a certain form of genius which is not incompatible with a vapour-filled mind.

Like a very true dandy, Mariano Osuna begins to shine by acquiring a polish. Later on attention would come, but for the moment he went unnoticed. He drew himself back to jump with greater force later. On his first visit to the dandies' lair he had very little contact with them. He was a mere delegate to the coronation ceremonies, and he saw only what he could glimpse over the heads of the diplomatic corps. He saw the dense pall that hung beneath Westminster Abbey's vaulted roof. A richly dressed throng filled the naves. An opening, the transept, covered by a flower-traced carpet. In the centre a chair of state in late Gothic and on the footstool a pair of stiff little feet. They belonged to a diminutive white queen, blonde, astonished, with her hair parted down the middle and two huge ear-rings on either side of her face. From the edge of her decolletage hung a long flower-embroidered mantle, embossed in heraldic designs. Other smaller designs were embroidered on the backs of her gloves. Sometimes she raised the sceptre, which rested upon her arm, like the palm of victory. She was surrounded by ladies-in-waiting, prelates, lords, generals, admirals, dignitaries. From amidst the rustle of laces, jewels, ermines, and gold-braid emerged a being in a long black cape and wearing a white wig. From a cushion he raised a crown surmounted by square crosses, and holding it aloft, advanced toward the chair; he held it in the air for a moment, and then let it descend until it clasped the tremulous brow of the fair little sparrow seated on the throne. From her temples a little tremor rippled down to the delicate border of her uncovered bosom.

XXII. AMOROUS INTRIGUE

Si je parle de l'amour à propos du dandisme, c'est que l'amour est l'occupation des oisifs. Mais le dandy ne vise pas à l'amour comme but special.

BAUDELAIRE

BACK in the Peninsula once more, Mariano Terranova performed certain services as Reserve Officer of the Royal Guard, and Gentleman-in-Waiting to Her Majesty, from June 1838, when he received the key.

In October of 1840 he went with his squadron to meet the royal pair at Provencio, on their return by way of Barcelona and Valencia. But as the company of the Guards was dissolved the following June, he was assigned to the Lusitania regiment, "with the rank of captain, the class of major, and the title of colonel," according to the complicated ranking of the day. By August thirty-first he was *de facto* colonel of the cavalry, and one after the other there appeared on his bosom the white cross of Malta, another of St. Ferdinand, the medal for distinguished service in the storming of Irun, and the medal of Our Lady of Villaviciosa, which was bestowed on him by the queen of Portugal, Doña Maria de la Gloria.

But, for the time being, he was somewhat surfeited with crosses and uniforms. By contrast he felt the attraction of that other sphere of society he had glimpsed while abroad, where certain men tyrannized over their fellow beings with only the magic art of properly handling a cane, a silk hat, and a pair of gloves. These were the aristocratic sleight-of-hand artists, the dandies who from Brummel down sowed "terror" and "attraction" in their wake, alternately enticing and repulsing Europe's glasses of fashion. The formula was a simple one: equal parts of irony "which is a corrosive" and wit "which helps dissolve it," to achieve this goal of foppery.

And, above all, the soul of a dandy was needed, and Terranova had it. All he required was a proper field for his operations. But early in 1841 he secured another leave of absence which permitted him to go to Brussels, Beauraing, and, on his way back, he set himself up in Paris for a time.

A keen taste for every form of enjoyment is already patent in the face of this insatiable devourer, whose life was consumed in squeezing out of existence every drop it had to offer. The folds around his eyes, his palpitating, sensitive nose, his full, sybaritic lips all reveal a refinedly sensual temperament which chafed at the barriers of prudence and position.

By rights woman should have been first in the order of his ambitions; but in reality, and in spite of his reputation, she was neither his sole objective, nor was she, strictly speaking, ever his prey. No, it is not true as has been said that the dandy should always be: *Alcibiade auprès des hommes et Don Juan auprès des dames.* The dandy never makes woman the exclusive goal of his impulses; for this reason he is not Don Juan. Woman passes through the outer circumference of his life, and from this contact a certain warmth is generated which either she uses to her advantage, as in the case of Osuna, or he, as in the case of D'Orsay.

It is true that women played an important role in Mariano Osuna's life; it is true that he was in love a number of times, and that he found himself involved in more than one intrigue from which he freed himself by resorting to flight, going abroad and pouring out riches in easy and amusing pastimes. But he never forgot who he was and did nothing unworthy of an Osuna, and in his own eyes, the only way he could becomingly behave, was by getting the worst of the bargain.

Osuna managed to make great success in love compatible with bad luck. He played the role of the man eternally pursued by beautiful women, the confirmed bachelor whose path was beset with charming, marriageable princesses. But as a matter of fact there were very few who loved him sincerely. In the long run it was discomfitures rather than triumphs this gallant reaped, and he resembled Don Quixote more than Don Juan. And like that knight he persisted unmoved in his pursuit of new failures, for "dandyism is a kind of cult of itself," says Baudelaire, "which can persist in its frustrated search for happiness in the exterior world, and especially, in women."

He was a gallant with women, a lover who sought not merely the satisfaction of the magnificent ornament which the prize of fair flesh constitutes for the coxcomb, but also that other intimate warmth which a hidden jewel may produce in the proper sensibility, as women sometimes wear a string of pearls inside their dress.

The ladies who in those days frequented the tables of Tortoni or the Maison d'Or in Paris began to notice, among so many French *nouveaux riches,* opulent South Americans, haughty Englishmen, and barbarous Russians, a Spanish gentleman who overwhelmed them with attentions, courtesies, and favours and who more than anyone else would have merited the judgments his countrymen had inspired in Madame d'Aulnoy when she visited Spain in the seventeenth century. She had marvelled at the way Spaniards made love and conducted their love affairs: *et sans compter les soins, la delicatesse, le dévouément même à la mort . . . ce que je trouve de charmant c'est la fidélité et le secret.*

And the same thing happened in his own country. A few years before certain elements in Madrid, offshoots of the famous groups of *El Parnasillo*—the cradle of literary and plastic Romanticism—and *El Solito* had formed a club in imitation of similar French organizations, which was located in the same neighbourhood in 1837. This was the origin of the

Casino of Madrid—situated first in the corner of the Calle del Principe and the Calle de la Visitacion, and afterwards, on the present site of the Comedy Theatre —where the young bloods of the day played billiards in their silk hats, and smoked around a brazier in a figure-eight wooden frame. Mariano Osuna was one of the first presidents. He had been preceded by the Count of Cumbres Altas and the Count of Montijo, whose fire-eating temper had made him famous in Madrid. Osuna was a frequent visitor to the Montijo country estate at Carabanchel and the palace of the Plaza del Angel, especially after the Count's death. He was attracted by the fascination of the beautiful shrewd widowed Countess of Montijo. That *brave femme*, the friend of Stendhal and Merimée, was one of the sharpest-witted women at the court. She was the mother of a brunette and a blonde—Paca and Eugenia —both extraordinarily beautiful, and she proposed to make suitable matches for them. To this end she worked out a most effective strategy. It was not unfitting that Mariano Terranova who had been on Córdoba's and Espartero's staff should now form a part of this other entourage. Time and again he was to be seen riding along on horse-back, leaning over to talk through the door of a landau returning from its drive down Trajineros, past the Fuente de la Alcachofa, and up the Cuesta de Atocha. Three women, all alluring, descended at the Plaza del Angel. Their escort often prolonged his visit in the house, playing charades with them or accompanying their songs or harp-playing at the piano.

At this time Eugenia Montijo, who was a mere child, had three aspirants on her horizon, and she hesitated between them: Mariano Osuna, Pepe Alcañices—the Duke of Sexto—and the Duke of Alba. Sexto was the best looking of the lot, the most dashing and the one she liked best. Alba did not displease her either. Mariano Osuna was only a second son, and besides he was so exaggeratedly polite with her that it put still more distance between them. Besides, strictly speaking, she was not the only one. They were three most desirable ladies and three gallants, and she noticed something queer between her mother and Mariano Terranova.

And, moreover, during the ups and downs of these friendships, mother Montijo had caught a glimpse of another possible suitor on the other side of the Pyrenees, "the taciturn prince," as D'Orsay had styled him, and whom Doña Manuela, making him the target of her maternal ambitions pertly called "Monsieur Isidore" when alluding to her future son-in-law in her correspondence with Merimée. Thus the destinies of France were decided by an astute match-making Countess and a sharp-tongued playwright. In 1841, in a letter to the Countess of Montijo, Merimée jested about the "belles cravattes de M. Téllez-Girón." Three years later, every time that he and Don Mariano were fellow guests at the table of the beautiful Countess of Merlin in Paris, Merimée feasted his eyes anew on his beautiful neckties and his pink pearl studs, and listened to Osuna's gusty sighs as he inquired about Paca Alba.

But not so the destinies of Mariano Terranova. Suddenly he departed, and unexpectedly appeared at the *cour des baisers* of the *Messageries Laffite et Caillard* to take a place in the diligence. As yet he had no private train nor post chaise of his own, as he was to have later on, but his second-son elegance had to be content with the best seat in the huge rattle-trap. In his broad-brimmed low beaver, his six-caped redingote, a leather bag, a pistol, a silk handkerchief around his throat, a carpet-bag at his feet in the straw that covered the floor, Mariano Osuna set out to see the world. There was the good earth offering itself to him through the little front window. Two vertical lines cut through the landscape obstructing the vast immensity of his flight, and accompanying the traveller with that same besetting parallelism which later on would be produced —horizontally—by the telegraph wires. Two lines, two bars, two reins suspended there over his head guided the destiny of this diligence which launched itself noisily down the highways. But *il mondo é poco* the swaying of the reins spelled out in space.

Part Four

THE GRANDEE OF THE GRANDEES OF SPAIN

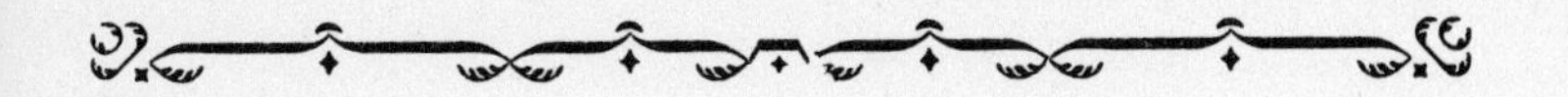

XXIII. THE DUCAL CORONET

L'orgueil persuade la presomption.

PASCAL

THE hand of fate has pulled a noose shut; the breath of life has been cut off. In the midst of his journey Mariano Terranova feels the horn of plenty break with a terrific blow over his head. His brother, the heir, has died suddenly. Mariano must return at full gallop in time for a hand to pass on to him, from the unsealed sepulchre, the torch which is later to burn itself out in his grasp. He reaches the court for the funeral and requiem masses. A treacherous fate that day laid before him all that he could most desire on earth, in exchange for snatching away his one real affection. And he becomes the head of his house.

On August 29, 1844, Mariano Téllez-Girón became, in his own estimation, the embodiment of everything desirable on earth. Upon his brow descended the Osuna coronet, with all its honours, privileges, rights, entailments, and all this as a natural, logical thing.

And yet, let us for a moment imagine a man who were suddenly to put on his forehead an ornate gold circlet, teeming with figures and battle-cries, in a confused conglommeration and uproar; and were to secure it there with the solemn gravity of one who fulfils a duty and exercises a right. Above the circlet rises an angel with full-spread wings, an eagle about to soar into space and a fiery steed plunging down from its heights. This man would be demented, or on the point of becoming so—but perhaps not: this man is simply a true aristocrat.

There are and always have been two completely different classes of nobles: the knight and the courtier. That is to say, the straight-backed nobleman and the back-bending nobleman.

The first feels his nobility in the indomitable independence of his blood, in his untamed, rebellious pride, as forbidding as the stiff outlines of his feudal tower, of his firm cuirass. He is the self-willed, turbulent lord who grudgingly acknowledges his sovereign's authority because his pride inclines him to the undisciplined *non serviam*. In a word, he prefers to be a "mouse's head rather than a lion's tail."

But no less high-born is the knee-bending courtier, "the lion's tail"; his pride of race expresses itself in his willingness to serve his master. He is the blue-blooded vassal, the steward, the gentleman-in-waiting, the palace official who puts all his nobility into showing his loyalty and feels honoured by his magnificent brocaded livery. He is the buckled noble as opposed to the spurred noble.

But there is yet a third degree of nobility which combines both tendencies: the aristocrat of highest rank. For he is his own vassal, the slave of his own name. He serves his own crown like something divine, which by the grace of God, through no merit of his own, has been placed upon his brow. He is the despot of an imaginary kingdom. Unlike a real king he has no responsibility, no liability. He fears neither conspiracies nor plots against him. He has only a name and a nominal cult of which he is the high priest. Nobody disputes his existence as nobody disputes that of the false gods, and he lives on an Olympus brilliant with age-old ceremonies.

This aristocrat is not the hidalgo; he is not noble because he descends from a king, a saint, or a hero. He is who he is; his lineage has always been the same. The true aristocrat is all that he is precisely because he cannot be more than he is. And in this sense it is doubtful whether there is a purer lineage than that of the Giróns, for, in reality, they have always descended from themselves and have been illustrious, more than because of their achievements, because of the accumulation of equally illustrious lineages. This explains the fatuousness of a man like Osuna who suddenly feels upon his feather-brained head a crown as rich in tinsel as poor in responsibilities. As God has created and tolerated a faulty world in order to achieve through it omnipotence in his own eyes, he who receives something without deserving it feels a divine impulse to risk it, to stake it all and win it back through his own efforts if he can.

Osuna, an aristocrat to the marrow of his bones, felt this divine impulse. But he played and lost. He lost what he played, true; but he won an everlasting coronet: the legend of the magnificent gesture raised to a philosophical category.

XXIV. THE VERTIGO OF THE ABYSM

C'est danse ce que l'on suppose le vide que se tiennent les assises de la Destinée.

SAINT-PAUL ROUX

MARIANO GIRÓN no sooner receives this crown than it goes to his head. He becomes the grandee possessed by the delirium of grandeur. Osuna, as Cocteau would say, was a madman who believed himself Osuna. He was a man possessed, possessed of himself, who ended in total dementia, in absolute derangement. To this torch-bearing madman his investiture seemed a dream, and he was continually attacking it to test its reality, its durability. There was no more legitimate title than that of Osuna since it had always been handed down unbroken in the strictest primogeniture. Nevertheless, he needed to inflate himself, and play a role for his own benefit; that is to say, prove his nobility by turning his reality into a farce.

Don Mariano Osuna came by his fatuity honestly. The insufferable vanity of the Benaventes was notorious, their sublime impertinence, their self-sufficiency, their airs; and it was in a Beaufort that the author of the *Maxims,* La Rochefoucauld, made his study of vanity. A libel of 1822 thus describes the Infantados: "Take equal doses of haughty pride and wealth, add a few drops of extravagance, and you have a Duke of the Infantado." As for the Osunas, one does not need to go back to the Grand Duke or to Don Pedro Girón, the famous Commander; any one of them will do, the fifth Duke, for instance, whom Madame D'Aulnoy knew during her voyage to Spain, and of whom she wrote afterwards: "The Duke of Osuna of the Girón family adores the ladies, and spares nothing to please them; he is a relentless enemy, and he has withal such an opinion of himself, such pride and such arrogance that nobody can endure him. Yet he can be most entertaining when he lays aside his airs and comes off his high horse."

The true-born aristocrat does not recognize inferior degrees of nobility. For him "the only privileges are those he enjoys." He is as much of a despot as the Emperor Paul I who said: "In Russia the only nobleman is the one I am talking to, and only as long as I am talking to him." And it was precisely in Russia that the Duke of Osuna's delirium of grandeur reached its culmination. There he was to find the most absolute monarch, the vastest domain, the most intense cold, and the cannon of highest calibre. There Osuna styled himself: "The Grandee of the Grandees of Spain."

He needed to make a spectacle of himself falsifying his authenticity and using titles which he did not possess: to be first, and above all unique. On the steppes of Russia, this invariably lonely soul regretted not being immensely alone, like the sea, far from anything that vaguely resembles it.

But splendid isolation is not always of easy achievement. Far off, in the kingdom of Castile, there was an aristocrat, the Duke of Escalona, who signed himself simply "The Marquis," because he was the Marquis of Villena, and because the Marquis of Astorga, who signed himself the same way, disputed his pre-eminence.

Yet it was not titles that His Excellency D. Mariano Francisco de Borja, José Justo Téllez-Girón and Beaufort, lacked: he was twelfth Duke of Osuna, seventh Count and fourteenth Duke of Benavente, fifteenth Duke of the Infantado, sixteenth of Gandia, fourteenth of Arcos, twelfth of Lerman, fourteenth of Medina de Rioseco, fifteenth of Bejar, and of Plasencia, Pastrana, Estremera, Monteagudo, Francavila, Mandás and Villanueva; Prince of Squilache, of Mélito, of Éboli; thirteenth Marquis of Peñafiel, of Távara, of Gibraleón, of Marguini, of Terranova, of Lombay, of Zahara, of Santillana, of the Cenete, of Almenara, of Cea, of Algecilla and of Argüeso; sixteenth Count of Ureña, of Fontanar, of Beaufort, of Mayorga, of Belalcázar, of Bañares, of Oliva, Mayalde, Osilo, Coguinas, Bailén, Casares, Saldaña, Villada, of the Real de Manzanares and of the Cid; Viscount of the Puebla and Alcocer; Baron of the baronies of Alberique, Alcocer, Alazquez, Gabarda and Ayora, in the kingdom of Valencia, of the Roca de Anguitola, with the overlordship of the city of Repollea and the town of Mendolea in Naples; Lord of the Encontradas de Curadoria, Sihurgas, Barbajia, Ololay, Barbajia-Seulo and Zicci, in the province of Cerdeña; First Voice in the Councils of the latter; Warden of the fortress of Simancas; Sole Patron, *insolidum,* of the church of Our Lady of the Assumption of the town of Osuna, of that of the city of Gandía, of those of Pastrana, Lerma and Ampudia; Grandee of Spain of the first class, Gentleman-in-Waiting to Her Majesty, etc., etc.

XXV. THE EIGHT-POINTED STAR

La pudeur a inventé les ornements.

JOUBERT

At heart Osuna was a timid soul, extraordinarily modest and shy. When he was awarded the Grand Cross of Carlos III on the twenty-eighth of April, 1845, he parapeted his heart behind it. Each new decoration was another shell to hang on his tattered pilgrim's garb in that mad pilgrimage in which he risked name and fortune through the hazards and fortunes of sea and sky.

But outwardly he was exuberant, dazzling, magnificent. He loved decorations, partly because of their glitter, but also as shields to protect his naked sensibility.

His was a soul that dramatized itself; but being

that of the true dandy, it aimed to attract by repelling and to maintain a respectful distance between his fierce modesty and the fascinated public he congregated about him. His soul was rent, like his coat-of-arms, and all the cloaks, ribbons, chains, and orders could not cover the gash.

One day when Don Juan Valera beheld Osuna arrayed in all his glory for some ceremony he wrote in his Correspondence: "The Duke was as dazzling as the sun, covered from head to foot with medals, collars, and ribands." Scornfully or otherwise the only thing to which Osuna could be compared was a luminous planet. But what else was he or did he aspire to be? Behold him at the end of his days, studded and hung with the most brilliant decorations, which he had set with splendid gems, and some of which had been specially created for him. Over his general's uniform he wore the collar of the Fleece of Gold, the Royal and Distinguished Order of Carlos III, the Grand Cross of the Supreme and Royal Prussian Order of the Black Eagle, as well as that of the White Eagle and the Red Eagle, with its diamond collar, and of the White Falcon of Saxe-Weimar. Mingled with the birds, the saints: the Grand Cross of the Imperial

Order of St. Alexander Newsky of Russia, set with diamonds; that of St. Stanislaus, St. Anna, St. Hermenegild, three of the first order of St. Ferdinand, that of St. John of Jerusalem, the chain of St. Andrew . . . and also the ribbon of the Imperial Legion of Honour of which he was an officer; the Great White Cross for Military Merit and the Royal Cross of Merit of the Golden Crown of Bavaria, and that of Our Lord Jesus Christ and the Immaculate Conception of Villaviciosa of Portugal, and of Our Lady of Guadalupe of Mexico, the Cross of Calatrava, the medals of the Royal Academy, the key of Gentleman of the Bedchamber, and ribbons, sashes, emblems, insignia, crosses received for action in war, etc., etc. And all assembled in a bizarre and dazzling confusion, completely covering his breast.

But he bears them all, distinguishes them and esteems them; he knows their value, their rank, their honours. They make a constellation about him as he moves, and he carries with him the puerile firmament of his colossal ambitions. Like a god with the stars, in the infinite spaces, he cherishes them, he contemplates them, and "he calls each one by its name."

XXVI. THE HORN OF PLENTY

Or with the princes that had gold who filled their houses with silver.

Job III, 15

A TROPHY won by Hercules in his fight with Aquelo, or wrenched from the head of the she-goat Amalthea in a fierce attack against a tree, was the horn which was to become that of Plenty when a nymph should offer it, overflowing with flowers and fruit, to the infant Jupiter. So goes the old, far-away myth.

To the thirst of a nineteenth century Spanish dandy the most exuberant cup that Spain possessed at the time was offered: the greatest fortune together with the most exalted rank. Osuna drained the horn to the tip and blew upon its emptiness a blast which deafened his contemporaries and still resounds in the legend which has come down to us. So runs the modern, close-at-hand myth.

It is said that Osuna could ride through half of Spain without leaving his own domains. In Don Mariano Téllez-Girón there came together "the greatest wealth and honours that any Spanish nobleman had ever possessed. The richest inheritances of the leading and oldest families of our country and of Belgium and Italy."

The figures of his income, twelve million reales in gold ($600,000), the size and quality of his estates, palaces, castles, art treasurers, etc., mean nothing unless one takes into account the difference of values between his time and the present, the cost of living, and the insignificant return on capital in those days. It is enough to know that hc inherited an income of over five million pesetas, and that the year he died he still had a credit of fifty million.

The palaces he inherited with their immense holdings are well-known: the Infantado palace in Guadalajara, with its carved stones and embossed ceilings; that of Beauraing in Belgium which dated from the twelfth century and which he completely rebuilt as it had been destroyed during the Revolution; that of the Mendozas in Toledo (afterward the Hospital of the Holy Cross); that of Arcos in Seville; that of Benavente which formerly had a zoological garden in its grounds; those of Gandía, Osuna, Bejar, Manzanares, Pastrana, etc., etc. In Madrid alone—besides the estate of Aranjuez and the marvellous Alameda just outside the city—he had several regal mansions.

The ancient palace of the Giróns had been built over the primitive walls of Madrid in the sixteenth century. In the nineteenth century the old palace of the Osunas, still "of great sumptuousness" was situated at one end of Leganitos street, over a riverbed, adjoining the famous garden of Las Minas, which in times of the Moors was known as *algannit,* from which Leganitos comes, and which means garden. This building later became a convent. The Benavente palace, on the Cuesta de la Vega, later became the French Embassy. Don Mariano took up his quarters in the Vistillas palace which he greatly improved. More than a palace it was a veritable group of palaces which he had inherited on the Infantado side. The Vistillas palace, which has since been demolished, was a huge edifice which his great-grandmother, a Princess of Salm-Salm, Dowager Duchess of the Infantado, had built across the way from the old Infantado palace, at the end of Don Pedro street. Later on, the library, armoury, and carriage rooms were installed there. Observers commented on the contrast between the severe exterior of the Vistillas palace, and the pomp of the inner courtyard, with its imposing statues of warriors, heralds and standard-bearers—"in the Faubourg St. Germain taste," says Mesonero—and the sumptuousness of the interior. "Its splendour," he adds, "leaves nothing to be envied in the palace of a sovereign." It was profusely decorated with precious carved woods, gold laminated doors, floors of marble and rare woods, hangings embroidered in silk, with valances, cords, rosettes and tassels after the fashion of the day. Tapestries, hangings, statues, armour, the richest of furniture filled the palace: in a drawing-room hung with red damask there was a Hebe of translucent Carrara; in other salons there were paintings by Titian, Tintoretto, Rubens, Teniers, Sanchez Coello. Here, the Christ of Alonso Cano; there, Ribera's San Jeronimo; portraits by Goya of Osuna, the Duchess of Benavente, their children, Urrutia, Ricardos, Lapeña, etc., besides the panels in the Alameda. In a gallery there were works by Van Dyck, Pantoja, Lawrence,

Antolinez, Carreño, Bayeu, Esteve, Carnicero, etc., and busts and portraits of the family's ancestors (Giróns, the Grand Duke of Osuna, the Princess of Éboli, Lerma, the Marquis of Santillana, St. Francis of Borja, Cardinal Mendoza, Infantados, Benaventes, Ponces and Estuñigas), and views of the family seats (the Alameda by Pérez Villamil; Beauraing by Perichc and Legrip), and scenes of glorious events, such as the Battle of the Sagra, in which Carlos Luis Ribera commemorated the origin of the "Girón" lineage. Collections of arms; the numismatic collection to which Don Mariano was continually making additions, and a curious collection of hunting and racing scenes in water-colours and engravings by Blanchard, Hull, Hunt, Harris, etc.

The rear façade of the palace ended in a series of terraced gardens, dotted with rustic pavilions, rocks, mossy grottoes, trailing plants, summer houses and Chinese kiosks, which descended from the palace to the foggy banks of the river.

The famous library, "veritably regal," which contained sixty thousand volumes and a priceless collection of manuscripts, was located in the old Infantado palace. Adjoining buildings housed the armoury and the stables and coach rooms with the magnificent saddle horses, post horses, and carriage horses, and the superb lacquered coaches, chaises, carriages, and trappings for gala occasions, as well as the refuge or asylum which the Duke installed for his old servants. Several blocks and streets as far as the Costanilla de San Andres, and the Plazuela de la Paja, including the old palace of the Lassos of Castile, which Duke Mariano restored, also belonged to the family. It was he who began the huge razing operation in what was the old Corral de las Naranjas, to make a square with gardens in front of his house, and he laid out an esplanade, which was destined to hold only vender's heaps of melons amidst whorls of dust.

Let us hear the description by Mesonero Romanos of the human ant heap which filled the palaces. Whoever went to see his Grace had to pass doorkeeper, footmen, ushers, and private secretary, past offices bearing such inscriptions as Secretariat, Pay Office, Archives, Treasury, Commissary, etc., etc., and which swarmed with people. "The occupations of these gentlemen were manifold: one plied his proficiency at fancy lettering, another, his elbows propped up on the desk and his lips tightly pursed, read the Gazette;

some were basking in the sun near a window; others, with their hands buried in their pockets, dozed in the easy-chairs; at eleven o'clock footmen came around with bottles and glasses and sandwiches which they all fell upon in order to restore their strength to serve His Grace."

And there were still other subordinate buildings adjoining the Vistillas palace, with offices, archives, and bureaus, gorged with employés and servants of the most varied aspect: from the frock-coat of the agent one passed through a series of liveries to the striped vest and black sleeves of the grooms. And if the first was an ex-Minister, the latter had been imported from England at a fancy salary. When all the obligations of the house are calculated, one must bear in mind that in spite of such great wealth, the vast fortune of the Giróns—time and again squandered and restored—was already somewhat insecure when it reached Don Mariano's hands. A loose thread hung from the rent. A tug from Don Mariano and the purple mantle was unravelled once for all.

In Osuna, the family-seat, the Giróns kept up magnificent chapels with an orchestra, choir, nine chaplains, etc., but the castle was falling to ruins. How were they to defend their patrimony with the ramparts crumbling away?

Close to Morón, a holding of the duchy, lies Osuna, called Oxuna by the Arabs, and Urso in time of the Romans, that is to say, bear. Its scutcheon displays two fierce plantigrades chained to the bars of a tower. There was likewise a bear on its currency: a bear standing on its hind feet, similar to that white one shot by Don Mariano in Russia, which stood at the foot of the stairway in the Vistillas palace, beside the gleaming sedan-chair, with a silver salver in its paws. A curious coincidence, this of the Andalusian Ursus and the bear of the steppes which was to rend it to pieces. With less justification the author of *Le Hazard et la Destinée,* M. J. Sageret, finds a parallelism between Clement XIV's "Ursus Velox" and the U.S.S.R. of the Soviet Republics. We merely point to the embrace of the nihilistic prince of the house of Osuna and the emblematic bear of the Slavic country.

XXVII. SIGNS OF THE TIMES

Parlant seul avec moi-même à deux pas de la mort, je suis encore hypocrite . . . O dix-neuvième siècle!
STENDHAL

As it passes, the baroque banner of Romanticism leaves behind it a complicated, intricate trail like the most delicate calligraphic flourish. Romanticism has falsified everything: "We have invented everything, even the Middle Ages," said Janin. Kings sit on imitation Gothic thrones. With the exception of Russia the courts were going through a period of strictest economy. Victoria of England and Christine of Spain lived modestly. Louis of Bavaria always said as he called for his hat: "Mine is the shabbiest." Louis Philippe left the throne asking: "Where are my keys?", and he called his son Montpensier *mon dépensier*.

But there were feudal nobles still. Osuna, for instance, who made his appearance as things were beginning to get out of joint. Sainte-Beuve said of the nineteenth century: *plus il avance en age, plus il se cottonise et s'affadit.* Nothing keeps its proper proportions: trousers are too long, coats too short; curtains lie in folds upon the floor, but the material in screens is too skimpy and strips and ruffles and borders have to be added. The most pretentious dining-room has a white inverted bowl in the centre which sheds a feeble light. Tables are covered with mats; chairs have tassels and fringes to hide their legs, not out of modesty, as in the gloomy days of Calvinism in Holland, but to dissemble the plain pine wood. What had been exuberant becomes ponderous. Velvet yields to plush and bronze to zinc; jardinieres make their way into the drawing-room; furniture is massed together, and intertwined; pictures in ebony frames repose draped upon easels, and lustre plates perch upon the walls. Nothing sits firmly in its place, nothing fits. It is a time of conspiracy and uprisings. The cape hides a multitude of sins, and from under the silk hat the revolutionary sideburns begin to emerge.

Things become hollow, pompous parodies of themselves. Only thus can they surmount themselves.

Chesterton defines caricature as a serious affair which manages to "make a pig look more like a pig than God Himself." It is the Satanic "I would have done a better job"; it is also the motto of snobs: "*affectation des affectations et tout est affectation,* exclaims Barbey d'Aurevilly, the personification of affectation.

Things are not esteemed for what they are but for what they seem; and they are worth nothing until their import is brought out in exaggerated spectacular fashion. This is the time when the great are no longer satisfied with the old family portraits but seek the services of the painter of historical scenes who turns them out in series, in dramatic attitudes. The genuine is falsified. Porcelain roses are introduced into the gardens because Nature should seem unnatural, and art supplant reality. Stone imitates stone, and brick, brick; walls are cracked and chipped by design. The world is growing frail; so much attention to appearances is turning it into empty decoration. What better setting than this for the frenzied drama of grandeur of the grandee among the grandees of Spain?

Osuna is the authentic comedian. Unlike the occasional farceur he has never a moment of relaxation. He is always in character, and always obsessed with himself. In his own eyes and those of his contemporaries —he would not really be the Duke of Osuna if he did not properly play the part. He must possess the gestures, the "business." "To be without seeming," said the Medici. "To seem is to be," said Barbey d'Aurevilly, "for the dandy and for women." And this is the preference of an age of acute Bovaryism, in which everybody envisaged himself as somebody else, an epoch that said: "Victor Hugo was a madman who thought himself Victor Hugo."

Chacun veut être un autre, says La Rochefoucauld. True. But when the one who wishes this already carries within himself the ambitioned goal, he finds himself hemmed in on every side, and like the superman, loses his reason. What more can one be than the Duke of Osuna, thinks Mariano Girón? And then in his delirium he falsifies reality, using titles, uniforms or decorations which are not his.

He had the right to the posts of First Gentleman of the Bedchamber, First Notary of Castile, or the abolished admiralty of Castile; he could have revived these or others, yet he used that of Prince of Anglona, which had been ceded to a collateral branch of the family; he retained the dukedom of Pastrana, disputing it with Don Manuel de Toledo, the son of the last Infantado, and on his delicately engraved visiting cards, he at times added in handwriting: "The Grandee of the Grandees of Spain."

On his passport he used the following names, in this order, which was not, strictly speaking the proper one: Téllez-Girón and Beaufort-Spontin, Pimentel, Fernández de Velasco, Herrera, Diego López de Zúñiga, Pérez de Guzmán, Sotomayor, Mendoza, Maza, Ladrón de Lizama, Carros, Arborea, Borja, Centellas, Ponce de León, Benavides, Enríquez, Toledo, Salm-Salm, Hurtado de Mendoza, Orozco, Silva, Gómez de Sandoval, Rojas, Pimentel, Osorio, Luna, Guzmán, Mendoza, Aragón de la Cerda, Enríquez, Haro and Guzmán.

In communications directed to him, the following forms of address were to be employed:

Sir:
Your Excellency.................................
....
God save the important life of Your Excellency.........
Excellent Sir.
Your most humble servant,
kisses the hand of Your Excellency.
Dated 18—.

His stationery was blue with the ducal coronet surmounted by the eagle, the angel, and the charger in relief. On the innumerable letterheads of his various possessions flourishes, curleycues, borders, and displayed initials abound. Everything about him was theatrical. He was never alone with himself; his position and title were always at his elbow. Besides there is his dandyism. "The dandy," says Baudelaire, "should aspire to be uninterruptedly sublime, should live and sleep before a mirror."

And here is the intimate and touching drama of a being who at one time seeks and flees himself. He knows that "a man's true dignity resides in what he is, not in what he has." And he is nothing less than Osuna. But he wants to be different Osunas, and in playing the Duke he unconsciously reveals what he lacks and what he desires.

To a fancy-dress ball Osuna went as Osuna; that is to say, as the Grand Duke with plumed hat, sword and Van Dyck collar. In the impersonation the name and some of the insignia were correct. But the collar of the Golden Fleece had not yet been bestowed upon him. And in order to wear it he disguised himself, and then had his photograph taken. On another occasion he attended a military review, and to his honorary foreign uniform he added the Spanish insignia and the white cape of Calatrava. And again he had himself photographed. And similarly, in all his iconography, one observes a childish, perhaps Pascalian, passion for outdoing himself, which makes him touching, and at times disturbing.

XXVIII. DUTY AND SERVICE

Il faut aimer sa place; si tu es roi, aime ton sceptre; si tu es valet, ta livrée.

JOUBERT

DON MARIANO received his political baptism on December fifteenth, when the province of Zamora elected him to Congress. Nevertheless, and notwithstanding the high offices he held, politics had no attraction for him; perhaps because he was unable to reconcile the creed of the class to which he was born with the overpowering instinct of rebellion within him. The world attracted him, with its pomp and its amorous and diplomatic tilts. Paris, aglow with the splendour of Romanticism's setting sun, called to him. There was a brilliant group of Spaniards there, Martínez de la Rosa, ambassador at the time, Sousa, the Marquis of Santiago, the popular Benjumea, the opulent Aguado, owner of the Maison Lafitte, of the Petit Bourg, and of a palace in the Place Vendôme, and Eugenia Montijo, just turned nineteen, whose ears still rang with the prophecy of Stendhal who, one day, when as a child he was holding her on his lap, prophesied that she would marry a great gentleman.

But whom? Osuna, perhaps? They had danced lancers and quadrilles hand in hand in Carabanchel, and she had already shown her preference for him over Arcicollar, Ayerbe, Molins, and Lema. She liked Alba, but he had settled on Paca, and Eugenia in her humiliation took a small dose of poison and lay down on her bed to die. But Death did not come, and the Duke of Sexto did, and then she decided to go on living, and it is even whispered that she always loved him, though she was convinced that his devotion was meant for Paca. As for Osuna, confronted at this time by such dangerous rivals as Aguado, the Marquis of Las Marismas, and even the Duke of Aumale, and Prince Luis Napoleon himself, later on, he did not ask for her hand. Why? He was one of the most sought-after matches in Europe. He was mentioned as the possible consort of Princess Louise Fernande, the heiress to the throne—and Eugenia Montijo, beautiful as she was, intelligent, calculating, and ambitious, was not enough for this colossal coxcomb—whom, it is interesting to note, the historians of the Second Empire all coincided in calling the Spanish Ambassador, for, if not in fact, his rank made him a *quasi ambassadeur*, as Arsene Houssaye would have said.

Back in Madrid the next year, he was made a Grandee, as Count-Duke of Benavente, and the infirm Duke of Frias, whose brows were clasped by an invisible laurel wreath, acted as his sponsor, as he had done for Don Pedro, the Frustrated, before Isabel II. On August 24 of the same year he was made senator in his own right. There was no summer vacation in those days; life went on without interruption. Congress, theatres, and dances continued as usual. The Royal Family moved to La Granja and Osuna installed himself in the Alameda, accompanied by his close friends, Nicolas Alcañices Corres, Ribadavia, and the unfailing squad of subordinates, the eternal footstool required by so many fine gentlemen.

Osuna shone brightly at the court that first year of his reign, which coincided with the festivities incidental to the double wedding of the Queen and the Princess: levees, receptions, fancy dress balls, soirées, theatres and bull-fights. The best of all was the bull-fight. It took place in the Plaza Mayor where the shabbiness was covered with painted canvas, and the balconies draped with tapestries and arrases, or crimson and gold hangings. Under a canopy of ruby velvet sat the royal couples in the Casa de Panaderia. In front of them, acting as a protecting wall, stood the royal guard of halberdiers, uncovered and in regular uniform. The mayor presides. When the Queen was in her place the nobles entered the square. The first was dressed in pale blue and white and rode in a carriage drawn by four bay horses. He alighted with his equerry, approached the royal canopy, bowed and saluted. The next was dressed in green velvet trimmed with white satin, and his gala coach was spanned with crimson harness. The third was also in green, and finally there rolled up slowly a majestic yellow carriage drawn by four chestnut horses decked out in red and yellow plumes. A knight dressed in crimson in the style of Philip IV descended; it was Don José Cabañas; after him came the Duke of Osuna; he wore a cavalry uniform, and he led Cabañas by the hand, to present him. After them came the matador, Francisco Montes, in his scarlet and silver suit, his bull-fighter's hat and his cape hanging from his arm. And then the troop of grooms, lancers, heralds in plumed hats, muleteers, picadors, the other members of the bull-fighting crew, etc., etc.

It was almost dark, and in the glow of six hundred blazing torches the silver ornaments of the three bull-fighters, Montes, Cuchares, and El Chiclanero, gave off metallic gleams as their shadows stretched out on the ground.

XXIX. FLYING ZEPHYR

Alcibiades proposed to enjoy the graces and luxuries of life again and teach the Spartans what their jealousies had lost for them.

E. F. BENSON

PRIMUS *et ire viam* was the war-cry of the Giróns, mounted on the fiery charger which reared itself aloft among the acanthus leaves of their coronet. The Osuna steed must always be the first, and sometimes it flies.

In 1832 in Madrid, Blanchard signed the photograph of a winning jockey for Osuna's collection. In the Alameda where the Osunas kept their racing stable and stud farm the first experiment in horse racing was made in 1835, with gentleman riders; it was undoubtedly the first time it was tried in Spain.

In 1841 the Osunas and other friends got together to found the Society for the Promotion of Horse Breeding and the first president was Don Pedro Alcántara.

Two years later they made their appearance on the track. The gentlemen brought their best horses and ran a few races along the banks of the Manzanares, to the great satisfaction of all concerned, until one day a gipsy came along riding a disreputable nag bareback, and beat all the thoroughbreds hands down. It was a dark day for the gentlemen. New blood had to be introduced.

So Osuna imported Zephyr, winning the race on April 23, 1843, against Guadalcazar's Pagoda. Zephyr was the first triumph, Zephyr opened the way. The gipsy's feat gives only a faint idea of the unpretentiousness of those races. Some discarded jewel of the Queen's or a saddle were the trophies for which they competed. Don Pedro brought the sport up to the European standard and gave it tone. He brought in stallions, and bought and raised thoroughbred English and Anglo-Arabian horses.

After his death Don Mariano continued the good work. He spent huge sums in acclimating horse racing in Spain. On his continual visits to Paris and London he frequented the Jockey Club, he bought winners and hired English grooms, stablemen, and jockeys. Like a new Alcibiades this stranger in his own land taught his compatriots the *joie de vivre.*

In 1849 the races were up to the standard Osuna had sought to give them. It is the tenth of May and through the gate of Castile strings of horses make their way toward the hippodrome of the royal Casa del Campo. It is the second and last gathering of the season, and a grey fog gives it quite a British air. The horn of a splendid tally-ho, drawn by six white-footed bays, announces the arrival on the field of the owner of the favourite stable: Osuna. At the first race he won both the prizes: the Queen's cup with Leda who did 3000 yards in two minutes, ten seconds, and the other with Lady Clementina, who beat Riansares' Radetsky. Today there is Queen Isabel's prize, 12,000 reales, and Clementina wins that, too, going three times around the track in less than six minutes. There is still another prize, that of the Society. In spite of the rain the interest is keen. The beautiful Duchesses of Alba, Frias, Sesa, and Fernandina stand up in their carriages. The winner, Esmeralda, a curly-maned thoroughbred, receives an ovation. She is led in by a fair gentleman in a silk hat, silk-faced frock-coat, whose face reveals satisfaction, a goatee, and a beribboned monocle. A jockey wearing a coat of Osuna's dazzling colours, pants in the saddle.

Besides being one of the founders of the Society for the Promotion of Horse Breeding, Duke Don Mariano was an honorary member of the club of Sanlucar de Barrameda, and owner member of the Equitation Club of Madrid. He owned the best racehorses. Piccadilly belonged to him, and Capricho, Clementina, and Esmeralda, who were winners in the next years, and formed the foundation of Figueroa's stables, which with those of Salvatierra, Alba, Bedmar, San Carlos, and Marchesi, the royal string of mares at Aranjuez, and some of the English racers like Brings, Lamb, and the Duke of Glusberg, brought the Spanish turf to the apex of its splendour, when of Osuna and his triumphs nothing remained but a tenuous flutter in the air.

But there was something more. In Vienna there is still a breed of white Spanish horses known by the name of "ring-openers," which Osuna took there from his stables, and which have been preserved in the imperial stables. They stand out in corteges and parades, these white, broad-chested, full-throated steeds, with their small sheep-like heads, which might have escaped from the Girón ducal coronet.

XXX. POMP AND CIRCUMSTANCE

. . . blind
By gazing on its own exceeding light.
SHELLEY

YES, dazzled by the effulgence which emanates from himself and from which he cannot withdraw his eyes. This is how the dandy goes mad, overcome by his own brilliance. Ever attentive to the effect he is making, he, nevertheless, goes about with his eyes half-closed, as much because of his Narcissan self-adoration as because of the dazzle of his own radiance. His head is held high, his air is solemn—a mixture of satisfaction and disgust and there is in his gesture that "majestic frivolity" which Barbey d'Aurevilly admired in the famous Prince of Kaunitz.

Nil mirari was the motto of Bolingbroke. Osuna added the haughty "Mas vale volando" of the Pimentels. Regard him, stiff, *soigné,* perfectly turned-out in the engraving Leon Noel made of him in Paris in 1849 when he was on the point of marrying the Countess of Teba who was living there. Regard his tightly buttoned waist, his impertinent near-sighted gaze hidden under the fatuous rampart of heavy, fleshy lids—like those the divine Morales painted—his mouth compressed to heart shape, his moustache twisted to a point above the tuft on his lower lip. A high head, somewhat flat in front, and very bald.

The fact that Osuna was bald as well as near-sighted was quite in keeping with the taste of the epoch. The impertinent monocle goes with shiny craniums, not romantic locks. From the time that Morny, the all-powerful, refused to wear a wig and started the fashion of jamming his hat down to his ears, "à la Morny," it was the height of fashion to be bald. Count Noé explained his baldness by saying he was so tall that his hair turned giddy and fell. The Russians, Orloff and Gortchakoff, were bald. But above all Morny, who was known as: "His Elegance the Count of Morny," like Sagan, "The Prince of Chic and Sagan."

A bald head and a cane: signs of the times. Stendhal tells how he bought himself a cane when he was going to visit a lady so as not to carry his hands behind his back, "like the pope," and to look like a gentleman of fashion. The cane was the dandy's sceptre. He twirled it between his fingers like a magic wand, and he used it of bamboo, malacca, willow, laurel, olive, cherry, orange, myrtle.

In those days one needed a great many of everything. Casal, the beau of Bourget, had more than a hundred pairs of shoes, which were kept in a glass case he termed his "library," as Des Esseintes called the one in which he kept his neckties. It was said of Osuna—among so many other things—that he never wore a pair of gloves more than once and that his specialty was trousers. Dandies, like scientists, tacitly divide the field among themselves. That of trousers belonged to Osuna; nearly all of them went with frock coats or tailed coats, and it is said that he had three hundred and sixty-six pairs, and that he remembered each one in making his selection to his valet. Whether true or not, it is intriguing to think of the foresight of a dandy who was unwilling to appear twice in the same pair of trousers during the year, and who even made provision for leap-year.

"Man is the only animal that dresses," says Marsan. But sometimes the dandy has the spirit of a collector, and his fancies may resemble that of an English lord who collected the larynxes of famous singers in glass bottles. Beau Brummel assembled a group of skilled workmen to manufacture his gloves, and distributed the fingers among them.

To be sure, "dandyism" does not imply good taste. Baudelaire was a beau of his day, the most talented of them all, a dandy in spirit and in soul. Yet this was his choicest attire: black trousers, patent leather shoes, white socks, red necktie, yellow and red handkerchief, silk hat, a peasant's blue blouse and pink gloves. Certainly a bizarre ensemble, but not haphazard on the part of the dandy, whose fundamental precept of behaviour is "always do the opposite of what is expected of you."

XXXI. MUNIFICENCE

Au nombre de mes divertissements j'ai oublié de vous parler d'une Academie de l'Histoire dont je suis membre. Elle est presque aussi amusante que la nôtre.

MERIMÉE

THE same Academy of History which seemed so amusing to Merimée in the year '53, had gathered the Duke of Osuna to its bosom on the thirtieth of April, 1847, as Honorary Academician, which he had been since January 6, 1845 of the Academy of San Fernando, and since the following, of the Royal Academy of Music and Declamation. The same year Anglona, Villahermosa, Frías, and Martínez de la Rosa were elected, and on the fourth of February of the following year (1848) Osuna took his seat, together with Sainz de Andino and Amador de los Ríos, as honorary member.

Years later when the Marquis of Ayerbe became a member, his maiden speech was the obituary of the Duke of Osuna. After referring to his military services, his acts of generosity, his gifts to the State, his waiving of salaries and rights, he said: "In exemplary unselfishness and patriotism he has never been surpassed by any other member of his illustrious race. A typical example of the old Spanish nobility in his chivalrousness, patriotism, and generosity as well as in his military virtues and his diplomatic abilities. So much so, that it is doubtful if anybody else in the present century has ever carried out more important missions with such pomp and splendour."

Yes, a unique example of the splendid Maecenas, the lavish rather than generous magnate, Don Mariano Osuna could adduce as his claim to entrance in the Academy that if he was not a historian, he was History. He represented names illustrious in his country's annals, and rich with glory's laurels. If his archives contained the account of St. Francis of Borjia's canonization and the records of the Grand Duke of Osuna's trials, in his library, considered the finest in Spain and perhaps of all the private libraries in Europe, there were Florentine manuscripts of the fourteenth and fifteenth centuries, the manuscripts of *La Belle Dame sans Mercy*, of *El Carro de las Donnas*, of *Le Roman de la Rose*, of the *Crónica Troyana*, of the *Misal Romano* of Cardinal Mendoza, the first editions of the Marquis of Santillana, a splendid collection of Bibles, among them the Complutense. There were autographed works of Bartolomé de las Casas, Launnay, González de Mendoza. There were over a thousand manuscripts and a hundred autographs of Calderón, Lope, Tirso, etc., with all of which, as early as the eighteenth century, the Dukes of Osuna had opened a public library containing over thirty-five thousand volumes, on the lower floors of the Leganitos palaces, in charge of various cataloguers and librarians.

Don Mariano took great pride in keeping up his standing as a Maecenas, and made handsome returns to the homage of artists, musicians and writers. Any example will serve as illustration. It was in October, 1850, that the lovely Countess of Teba gave the bullfighter, Salamanquino, who had presented her with the knot of ribbons he had snatched from the bull, a rich cape of green cloth, trimmed with gold and embroidered by the famous needlewoman, Regina López;

about this same time Osuna presented the celebrated musician Barbieri with "a magnificent set of studs for shirt and waistcoat," for having dedicated his operetta *Tramoya* to him. Pirala and Alverá also dedicated their compositions to him, and Chamorro's exhaustive study of *Army Leaders* was handsomely subsidized by Osuna, though he refused to supply any information for his own biography, in spite of his excellent service record.

Another curious detail belongs to the same year. In the days when Christmas cheer deafened the streets, and the annual exhibition of cakes and sweets was held at the sign of *La dulce alianza,* the billboard of the Teatro Español announced the première of a particularly tragic, solemn, distressful drama in verse. It was by D. Juan de Ariza, and entitled *The First Girón,* and it was dedicated by its author to the Duke of Osuna. The cast included Teodora Lamadrid, Calvo, Pizarroso, Valero. The twenty-fourth of December was a night of triumph and success. There was one empty box. It had been presented to the Duke of Osuna, who, unable to attend the performance, sent a letter of regrets, enclosing two thousand-real

($50) notes. Among noble souls no calling is demeaning. The Duke received an answer from the leading members of the cast thanking him for the gift, and adding that they had distributed it among the members of the company, for "as for themselves, they were amply rewarded by Your Excellency's letter."

Unstintingly Osuna responded to every demand, enriching his galleries, his library, his coin collection; he ordered a History of the House of Osuna from his chronicler, Don Basilio Sebastian Castellanos, who began the work and never, so far as can be ascertained, completed it. The following instance serves as an illustration: in 1851 a poet brought him some verses he had written and received a gold piece and a silver cigarette case. Needless to say, Osuna was deluged with dedications: Don Fernando Doliac, a play; Amador de los Ríos, the magnificent edition (1852) of the works of the Marquis of Santillana, which the duke paid for, and Sales and Garcés the drama entitled, "The Test of Loyalty or the Duke of Bourbon in Toledo," which deals with the same valorous act of the Count of Benavente, which inspired the ballad of the Duke of Rivas, author of *Don*

Álvaro. The Duke of Osuna gave his forbears no cause for complaint; true, he squandered their patrimony, but it all redounded to the greater glory of their name.

XXXII. THE GOLDEN FLEECE

En fait d'inutilités il ne faut que le nécessaire.
CHAMFORT

Tittle: Sometimes I just feel like kicking everything into the middle of next week, beginning with this silly world.

Tattle: Be quiet and have patience. You shouldn't have been born the foot of a console table.

Tittle: To be a golden lion, to hold in my paw a world of gold and on my back a marble slab with statues, mirrors, carvings, and—

Tattle: Well, what did you expect? You're neither a lion, nor gold, but just a chunk of carved wood, like ever so many others, to ornament the royal chambers. But we are in a good position to hear all the underhanded scheming that goes on in the palace.

Tittle: Maybe you are. But here I am turned around to the left like this, where all I can see is the corner, and the flunkey's white stockings, a window, and a little piece of a mirror which just barely reflects the tricorne of a king dressed for the chase, and one of Tiepolo's clouds, from which there hangs a chandelier heavier than the royal coach.

Tattle: You can see the parade.

Tittle: It's the same thing every day, at the same hour. A sword that glitters in the sun, a bit of music that says good-morning to another bit, and an occasional blue pigeon that pecks round under the horses' hoofs.

Tattle: Be still, I can hear the rustle of a skirt and the click of a pair of spurs.

Tittle: What are they saying?

Tattle: Keep quiet.

Tittle: What's up?

Tattle: There's a heavy sea on, intrigues, fishing in troubled waters, all for the conquest of the Golden Fleece.

Tittle: What do you mean?

Tattle: They are making up the honours list. From what they say there are three vacancies for the

Golden Fleece, and they are going to award them in celebration of the Queen's delivery—God save her. One is for Alcañices, one is for Isturiz, and the other hasn't been decided. Apparently—I can't hear very well—yes, that's it, the Queen—God save her—is determined that it shall go to Bravo Murillo. He doesn't want it. She has ordered Miraflores to bring her the decree to be signed. The prime minister finds it out, rushes to the palace and pleads that this great honour be given to "someone more worthy of it"—those are his very words. Her Majesty consents. A name is sought that will satisfy everybody, and that of the Duke of Osuna is the evident choice.

Tittle: Is that all?

Tattle: They're leaving. There's a little of the binding ripped off the skirt. . . .

But in spite of all the tittle-tattle Osuna had to wait eight years—he would not ask for it—before he was granted, by a royal decree of November 16, 1860, the collar which the other Dukes of Osuna had displayed. The award was made with all the ceremony required by the occasion.

XXXIII. THE WORLD AS IMAGE

Le diable a ses martyrs.

J. Maritain

THE nineteenth century had entered upon its second half, and in one of the newspapers of Madrid one could read the following item: "Yesterday, at the usual hour, there were put to death, etc." But society —high society, naturally—kept on just the same with its round of bull-fights, concerts, dinners, drives, theatres, and fancy dress balls, at which the aristocrats displayed the arms and costumes of their illustrious ancestors.

Osuna, who belonged to the inner circle, accompanied the Queen wherever she went in a post of honour. Nothing took place without him: the opening of Congress, a banquet at the Papal Embassy for the new cardinals, the initiation of a new member in the Order of Calatrava, a visit of the Dukes of Montpensier to the Alameda, the inauguration of the Royal Theatre opposite the palace.

Naturally he could not fail to be present at this latter event in view of the tradition of music and *bel canto* which characterized his family. When *La segunda dama duende* was presented at the Montijo's country place about the middle of September, Osuna took part in it with Paca and Eugenia, and in the final chorus he accompanied the ladies on the organ which, from all reports, he played very well. On the night of November twentieth he was one of the first arrivals at the opening of the royal coliseum. The hall was dazzling, the gas lights gleaming on the red velvet and bright gold of the boxes. The seats which ordinarily sold for twenty-four reales brought three hundred and twenty that night. The Dowager Queen maintained that the new theatre was the equal of the San Carlos at Naples and La Scala of Milan. As the performance began a shower of little folded notes fluttered down over the audience. They contained poetical compositions in praise of Her Majesty signed by Selgas, Cañete, Bretón, Vega, etc. Donizetti's *La Favorita* was given and heard with great enthusiasm. The singers received ovations: Gardoni in *Spirto gentile,* Alboni in *Oh mio Fernando.* At the end of the performance the house got to its feet to cheer the Queen. Muffled in their capes the spectators left the foyer, satisfaction gleaming in their eyes, and with handkerchiefs pressed against their lips to keep out the sharp night air, which nipped at their ankles. The blue transparency is rent by the last coloratura, the shouts of the idlers who have been hanging about, to call the coachmen: "Osuna," "Frías," "Medinaceli" . . .

XXXIV. THE QUEEN WOUNDED

Who does not esteem his calling never distinguished himself in it.

QUEVEDO

THE second of February of the year 1852.

The Duke sits in his low, comfortable easy chair in a small, cosy drawing-room which looks out over the gardens of his Vistillas palace. Outside the cold is roseate. Night falls early. The Manzanares disappears from sight, swathed in its mists. There is one single purplish cloud. The façade of the Royal Palace is a congealed, consternated white. The sky, hemmed in by the Guadarrama's sierra, billows in space like a full sail, so tense that here and there in it unperceived stars pop through. Inside, warmth and tobacco smoke. The Duke combs the fringes of the chair with his hand. He rests his forehead on the other hand, with an air of fatigue and depression. Something has upset him. His gaze is lost in space, but it does not wander far from the palace. With him is Sanz Barea, a close friend who is keeping him company, a dandy of the day, the boon companion of great gentlemen, who describes the scene for us. The servant has brought in coffee (the secret fabricator of a rational frenzy, as Campoamor called it). Barea is waiting eagerly. Two bright black eyes gleam impatiently in the coffee cups. Finally the Duke begins:

"The first moments were terrible because we did not know how serious the wound was. When we are acting as escorts, we keep watch from the tail of our eye as we pass the galleries to make sure we're not getting out of place and spoiling the line. That's how I happened to see everything, and yet I can't quite realize what took place."

"Like a bull-fight: the matador is wounded and nobody knows how it happened."

"Exactly. I saw the priest. I saw him rush at the Queen; I saw her fall back and raise her white glove covered with blood."

"Then they were returning from the chapel?"

"Yes, just as we were moving toward the front stairway."

Here the servant announces Don Modesto, a reporter, who, once in a while, has sensational inside information for the Duke.

"Show him in." And turning to the newcomer: "More stale news?"

"Not stale, Your Grace. I know what happened as well as Your Grace himself, though you did overpower the assassin."

"Let's hear it then, and Heaven help you if you make a mistake."

And poor Don Modesto relates with a great wealth of detail all the particulars of the attempt: how Merino presented a petition to the Queen, how he said, "Take that," as he plunged his dagger into her; how she screamed: "My daughter! My daughter!" as she felt herself wounded and separated from the little princess; how one of the officers of the halberdiers raised the child high into the air so everybody could see her; how the Queen fainted, and in all the confusion Osuna, Alcañices, Pinohermoso, and Tamames pinioned the assassin down and prevented him from dealing a second blow. Then he describes the panic in the galleries, the swoons, the shrieks, the trampled feet, the shawls torn.

"And what happened in the royal chambers?" interrupted the Duke.

And Don Modesto went on till he got to the Queen's: "I forgive him; I don't want him killed on my account." Then he went on to give all sorts of details about Merino, his life, his plots, and wound up by revealing that the crimson mantle Isabel II was wearing was a copy of one of Queen Victoria's.

"Very good," interrupted the Duke, and holding out a gold piece he added: "That's what I call finding out things."

"Thank you, Your Grace. Won't I make them sit up and take notice at the café!"

"At the café? Didn't you tell me that you owed money there? Are you going to have the courage to go there?"

"Ah, Your Grace, when they see this kind face of our Sovereign,"—tossing the coin in the air—"it will soften their hearts."

And he bows and scrapes himself out of the Duke's presence.

Five days later the body of Merino burned on a pile of faggots.

XXXV. A SALVO IN ATOCHA

Quelque chose que l'on fasse à Madrid, pourvu qu'on aille dans un lieu public, on est sur de recontrer les même trois cents personnes.

MERIMÉE

DOWN Alcalá street, toward the Fuente Castellana, rides the cream of Madrid society: the Duchess Angela de Medinaceli, the Duchess Paca de Alba, in their carriages; the Countess of Vilches, on horse-back, followed by a groom, etc. On the sidewalks the pedestrians move along, silent and muffled in their capes, with the air of conspirators. The billowing folds of the capes brush against the water venders' trays. Suddenly a bugle calls. Behind the gratings of the Ministry of War the soldiers snatch up their guns. They form ranks, fall into line—like drawings in a child's picture book—and present arms. The procession is coming; a carriage "a la gran Daumont" flanked by swords and plumed helmets break through the afternoon. The bust of the Queen bows regularly to right and to left, and passes quickly, in time to the horses' rapid trot. Behind the bodyguard, the guard of honour. The Duke of Osuna rides in the second carriage, his legend floating behind him like a bright serpentine.

He is not merely a courtier, he is a soldier and a diplomat as well. And not merely a soldier of parades, either; he can count his campaigns. A brigadier-general since May 1, 1848, he has served with Villahermosa, Echagüe, Quesada, Moriones, Losada, Martínez Campos. His cousin, the Prince of Anglona, was Lieutenant-General at the time. Osuna had no command. On June 25, 1852, he was made Field-Marshal, and four months later he began his diplomatic career, representing his country as head of the commission that went to London to attend Lord Wellington's funeral ceremonies. He travelled in style; postillions rode ahead of him; his servants and luggage followed him on the highways in post chaises. But when he reached the shores of the Channel he had to pass the camel's eye which Albion, the well-fortified, makes all her visitors go through: the gang-plank of the flat-bottomed stern-wheeler, which takes eight long hours for its stately passage from Calais to Dover.

The Duke of Ciudad-Rodrigo, though his star was already setting, was treated like a sovereign in England. When he left the incense pall of Westminster Abbey behind him, he brought back, as souvenir of his first embassy, an oil painting by Sir Thomas Lawrence, a bust and other engravings by Greatbach and Faed; he hung them in his palace, and reports began to drift back of the astounding munificence and splendour with which the mission had been conducted—all the expenses came out of Osuna's pocket—and the good impression thus made.

With these gold sovereigns he threw into the Thames—figuratively speaking—Osuna laid the cornerstone of his legend. A little later on he would complete the structure by throwing—literally this time—dinner services of gold into the Neva.

Back in Madrid again, in February of 1853, Osuna was made Vice-President of the Upper Chamber. Attendance at the Senate made it necessary for him to live for a while in the capital. But Madrid bored him;

life was dull, he had to stifle his yawns. The Montijos kept on with their theatricals, and Merimée tells how that year Osuna was called Apollo in the plays they performed because he was always surrounded by nine women; but he adds "of the nine muses, unfortunately five of them are mothers or aunts of the other four," and describing a bull-fight with dogs, he writes "les taureaux n'ont plus de cœur et les hommes ne valent guère mieux."

Osuna's eyes are looking beyond the Pyrenees. The Countess of Teba—everything is over between them—is doing the same. When the news of her marriage to the French Emperor was announced in a theatre, a charming countrywoman of the Countess' jumped to her feet, exclaiming: "There's no future for a person in this country."

Osuna shared the opinion of these sagacious ladies of Granada. His prow was headed toward Europe, and soon he was to embark, in his magnificent galleon, with all sails set, on the perils of the European seas, leaving behind him shabby, poverty-stricken Spain, where the royal frigate was foundering, while the Queen danced polkas and mazurkas with her gigolos, Pontón, Villadarias, and Fernandina.

XXXVI. "SI NON E VERO"

Moi, comédien si souvent involontaire.
BARBEY D'AUREVILLY

ABOUT this time the news began to spread through Madrid of the unheard-of splendour with which Osuna was honouring himself and his country abroad. Making a legend of him, in spite of his proximity, the people incarnated their generosity in him, glad to find in a fellow-countryman the patron saint of their romantic aspirations. Reality is distorted to forge a type and a legend: an eternal figure comes into being. For this reason, although many of the things told about him are not true, they are authentic, for they engender a myth. The same thing may be said of him as Papini wrote of Ashaverus, the Wandering Jew: "The legend is not corroborated by any text . . . but it is true, with a truth greater than the historic."

But there are texts that talk of Osuna. One writer of the day says that the Alameda "is a most extravagant caprice, and with all its beauty is one of the abysses down which the patrimony of the illustrious house of Osuna is slipping away." And to be sure, the Duke kept it up with a lavishness seldom seen. It was not merely the necessary running expenses (in the neighbourhood of $50,000), but the hordes of visitors who came every day to see the place. The invitation cards gave them permission to ride about in the carriages, row in the boats, swing in the swings, etc., and eat in the palace where every day a sumptuous meal was served, presided over by the agent.

And the same thing took place in all the houses and palaces which the Duke had open in Spain and outside of Spain. Whether it was because, as some say, one day he arrived unexpectedly at one of them and found no meal ready, and ordered that in the future dinner was to be served everywhere, even if he was not there; or to imitate traditions legendary in the family, the point is that this is the way it was done, and there is authentic testimony thereof. Perhaps it came from the inner conviction possessed by every great lord that his most unsuspected desires should always be anticipated, for strictly speaking, a great lord may refuse or accept, but he should never request the least thing from anybody, not even a subordinate, and he suffers if he has to. "In spite of being who I am, I have never had a thing without having to ask for it," wrote Don Pedro de Alcántara, the Frustrated, bitterly in a letter.

Thus it is told of the Duke of Doudeauville, a contemporary of Osuna, that he had given orders that his carriages should be spanned every day; if, when they were announced, he did not intend to use them, he merely said *"Detellez."* And of Mariano Osuna it is said that his carriage went to the station to wait for him every day, and there it stayed, the liveried coachman drowsing in his seat, even though it was known that the Duke was far away, and was not expected, on the mere possibility that he, or a relative or friend might happen to need it.

The great lord is the sun; he does not live for himself, but that others may live. At the banquets which were served at the Vistillas palace in his absence, Alcañices or Herrero presided, and relatives, distant and near, and friends gathered at his board. In Paris many of the habitual diners at his table had never had the pleasure of meeting him. He could truthfully have said what Sagasta remarked to his wife: "There are people at our dinners whom I do not know, and I suspect many of them do not know me either."

Osuna offered the right of asylum in his palaces, and people ate and danced there, even though he remained in his rooms. All his palaces housed guests of the highest aristocracy, including royalty. In 1862 the King and Queen visited him at Bailén, and the reporter wrote: "Everything was amazingly rich and lavish, astonishing even those who knew that the house of Osuna would outshine itself on such an occasion." There was a baron of original ideas, about this time, who organized a splendid hunt on his estate at Biarritz, which he attended, wearing his red hunting coat, and comfortably seated on the highest terrace of his palace.

Osuna always travelled in a private train, and it is told that, if as he was on the point of departing, he happened to think of something he had forgotten, he had his majordomo bring it after him in another private train. If a pearl stud happened to fall from his shirt bosom, he never bothered picking it up, and he gave it to whomever found it. But it is not true that he wore diamond buttons loosely sewed on, so as to lose them and thereby add new fuel to the embers of his legend.

One day he happened to be in Madrid. He gathered his friends around the long damask cloth which bore the Osuna arms in filigree. He talked with this one and that, barely tasting the dishes that were set before him. Suddenly there was a pause in the conversation. His attention was attracted by the necktie one of his guests was wearing. He admired it and inquired where it came from.

"I bought it in Paris. It's an inexpensive thing."

Osuna made a sign and from among the bevy of liveried servants one dressed in black evening clothes approached. The tables had not yet been cleared before a servant of the house had departed in a special train for Paris to find another tie just like it.

Osuna's was a grandiose style. Gold pieces were common tips in his palace. On the margin of a note from his agent, which he had read and approved, it says: "I ordered the porter to receive a gold piece as a tip, for I wanted *to do things properly,* as we always do." *To do things properly,* that was his obsession and his guiding principle, which he followed, let it cost what it would. He had no choice; he had to do things in his own style, even though it involved heroic sacrifices.

To the legend of generosity and splendour he owed his fame. True, facts do not always fit in with the legend's requirements. But what does that matter. The myth must nourish the legend, as truth feeds history. If he did not do everything that was said of him, he gave grounds for saying it. The hero does not acquire fame by merit, but by conquest, often by violence; and he responds to his fame with further creation. It is known of Bayard that he had three natural children, yet he will always be, because he won the title by right of conquest, *le chevalier, sans peur et sans reproche.*

Monetary units of twopence and threepence were in use in Spain. It was easy to acquire a reputation there as a spendthrift and astound the court with coloured illuminations in which "barrels of oil" were used, on the occasion of the royal weddings. But where he won his fame was in France, where after the penury of Louis Philippe, the Second Empire had embarked upon a period of the most reckless extravagance.

The world in which Osuna shone was the one in which the Prince of Sagan once sent a lady camellias that cost 25,000 francs; where the Duke of Morny left a stable of one hundred and forty horses when he died, and where the lovely Countess of Pourtalès spent 8,000 francs on flowers to decorate her house for one night.

XXXVII. AN IMPERIAL SWEETHEART

. . . en ce Paris, où tous peinent et s'efforcent à faire semblant de s'amuser.

COMTESSE DE CASTIGLIONE

It was not a ducal coronet that an abbot had foreseen in Eugenia Montijo's hands, but that of Empress of the French. It was offered her by Louis Napoleon, the disdained "Taciturn Prince," to whom the European courts had refused their princesses of royal blood. They would not refuse them to Osuna, who years later, when on the brink of physical and material ruin, was to marry a lovely young Serene Highness of the house of Salm-Salm.

Installed in the Elysian Palace, which had once belonged to Madame de Pompadour, Eugenia completed her preparations, and surrounded by flowers and jewel cases, gave the last touches, with Palmira, to the interminable theory of new dresses which rested impassibly on wicker forms, like Bluebeard's beheaded wives. In an adjoining room Merimée, the go-between and amanuensis of the intrigue, who had leaped into space "clutching the parachute of the imperial crinoline," was, in turn, giving the last touches to the marriage contract. In drawing it up he had employed all his astuteness, accumulating names and titles which were designed to exalt the rank of the fiancée. Over his shoulder, the tender solicitude of Doña Maria Manuela prompts him with details. Everything must be turned to advantage, even former admirers. And the first of the bride's witnesses, together with the Marquis of Valdegamas—that famous Donoso Cortés, ambassador of Spain at the time—is the Duke of Osuna who signifies more in Europe than Louis Napoleon himself.

And Osuna accepts graciously, without rancour—he is the soul of generosity—and without resentment. He had not married the bride himself because he did not want to, but he made everybody believe the contrary. And though, up to then, he had resisted the seductive charm of this superb woman, when he saw her dressed for her wedding ceremony, all aglitter like an icicle, he felt himself once more under her spell.

On the twenty-ninth of January of 1853, in the Salle des Marechaux of the Tuileries, the civil ceremony was effected. Osuna stood beside the First Notary, the Minister of State. His air was solemn, his breast steady beneath the gleams of his decorations; but when he stepped forward to sign the register, after the imperial family and the cardinals, and received the pen from the hand of the Spanish Ambassador, a slight tremor can be discerned in the signature he inscribed there.

The religious ceremony was to be celebrated the following day: a wintry Sunday with ensigns and banners snapping briskly in the air. Above the festive multitude there floated on banners and wreaths a flock of crowned eagles quartered with a swarm of golden heraldic bees. The procession got majestically under way. The witnesses were riding in the carriage of honour: the Duke of Osuna, the Marquis of Valdegamas, the Marquis of Bedmar, General Álvarez de Toledo, the Count of Galve, brother of the Duke of Alba. Suddenly the procession came to a halt. What had happened? Nothing: as it passed under the arch of the Tuileries the coronet on the roof of the imperial carriage had rolled to the ground. Everything was fixed up, and the coronet put back in its place once more. The cortege resumed its march. But there were those who regarded it as an inauspicious omen, and recalled that at the same spot and under analogous circumstances the same thing had happened when Napoleon I and Maria Louise, riding in the same carriage, were on their way to their religious ceremony.

But who pays any attention to omens? The improvised court was on fire with luxury and extravagance, and in a blaze of festivals. It was a turbulent, unsettled court which wore too transparent clothing and talked too stridently. Everything was haste, confusion, boldness. For example, the Duchess Colonnia de Castiglione, in order not to be mistaken for the other Castiglione—the beautiful Nicchia, the "divine" and dubious Countess—had no scruples about saying to the footman of the Tuileries as they were about to announce her: *Annoncez la laide!*

The painters and engravers of the day tried to capture the fleeting moment of this whirlwind: Winterhalter, Hebert, Dubufe, Lami, Guys, and Dévéria cannot manage it all, so great is the turbulence of this radiant Paris, "the cabaret of Europe," as Pauline Metternich called it. The most extraordinary beauties shone and vied with one another: the Countesses of Pourtales, of Deaulaincourt, of Le Hon, of Castiglione, Walewska, Mercy Argenteau, the Marchionesses of Gallifet, Labedoyere, Las Marismas, and the Duchesses of Mouchy, Persigny, Cadore, and Sofia Valera, Duchess of Malakoff, an Andalusian like the Empress, and like her, beautiful and without prospects until an old marshal of France offered her his laurels and his fortune. And among them, eclipsing them in luxury and arrogance, the famous professional beauties: Cora Pearl, la Barucci, la Païva, Adela Courtois, Ana Deslions . . . whose magnificent carriages were to be seen, like those of the others, in the Bois de Boulogne, through the Champs Élysées, on the fashionable drive: *le tour du lac.*

On horse-back or in their carriages—the master himself often driving, a short blanket over his knees, and whirling the whip about in his hand to control the traffic—went the beaux of the day: Sagan, Grammount-Caderousse, Gallifet, Morny, Massa, Seymour, D'Alton Shee, Demidoff, and the famous Spaniard, the Duke of Osuna.

For the moment Osuna was living in Paris. Perhaps it was to be near the Empress rather than because of the tasteless splendour of the court. He also felt under obligations to a country which had honoured him with its distinctions, one day making him a Grand Officer of the Legion of Honour and another, Honorary President of the African Institute.

XXXVIII. THE HUNT IN COMPIÈGNE

Je crois qu'il n'a jamais éxisté un temps où le monde ait été plus bête qu'a present.

MERIMÉE

It is told of a Spanish lady of the day that, on a certain occasion a friend told her that he could see a bit of her leg under her crinoline as she bent over. Whereupon she answered:

"Is that so? Well, look at it and keep quiet."

The fashions of the epoch elicited from the disillusioned author of *Clara Gazul* such comments: "I saw a number of lovely legs and garters during the waltz."

The coy frivolity of the court is attested by numerous ancedotes of the Duchess of Castiglione, and of the Empress herself, especially somewhat later, in Merimée's letters from Compiègne to an unknown lady, in which, after going into raptures over the jasmine and tuberoses, he speaks of a work of his that has been performed as "a wee bit immoral."

The imperial court disported itself in Compiègne, and its amusements gave rise to childish scandal. All sorts of stories were told about the amazing diversions with which the sovereigns regaled their guests. As a matter of fact the orgies consisted in dancing to the jangle of an automatic piano and playing charades in the Map Room. During the autumns of 1855 and 1856 these entertainments were notoriously brilliant. The invitation lists were made up with great care and included aristocrats, writers, members of the middle class, and the "inevitables" (high officials and dignitaries); in this way Verdi, Meyerbeer, and a moody, brusque young gentleman, Alfred de Vigny, soon to die like his wolf, in silence and alone, mingled with ambassadors and the Papal representative. Osuna at this time was creating a sensation with his display of wealth and elegance among the ladies gathered at Compiègne: the Princesses of Beauvan and of Poniatowska, the wife of General Serrano, the wife of Marshal Magnan, the Duchess of Lesparre, of Istria, and so many others mentioned in the chronicles of the day.

The specialty at Compiègne was the hunts. The Zouaves on guard acted as beaters and raised up brown clouds of partridges. There were days in which three thousand were killed with ten guns. One of the best of these was Osuna's, who, attended by three or four gillies, in livery, bandoliers and tricorne or green velvet caps, could be distinguished in his post by his buttoned jacket of leaf-brown corduroy, knicker-bockers, high leggings, and his broad felt hat with its pheasant feather.

There were other famous guns among the visitors: Lord Cowley, Metternich, the Duke of Beaufort, the Duke of Manchester, the Duke of Atholl, Lord Palmerston, Strafford-Canning, Herford, and the Emperor himself, a crack shot.

Sometimes the Empress took part, but as a rule she preferred the archery contests on the left side of the wood. But she always presided from the great window of the principal courtyard over the ceremony known as the "cold bait" on the days of the deer-hunts. It took place in the dark of night with only the uplifted torches of the liveried, white-wigged footmen for illumination. On one side lay the offal of a deer, covered by the skin and the head. On the other the eager pack, raging to plunge at it. An upraised whip held them back. The air is rent by the metallic horns of the hunters and the frantic barking of the pack. Every time the whip is lowered the open-mouthed dogs try to hurl themselves upon the bait. But the whip is raised again until it is finally lowered and the "Hunt, halloo" rings out. The air is rent with howls, whipcracks, snarling as the horns blare out their notes, and the crowd rushes off, lighted by a strange flickering green light which arouses the wonder of the spectators.

Osuna is not taken in by these gleams. He knows that they are produced by copper salts. Just as he knows that nearly everything that decorates the drawing-rooms is plaster, and that every spoon on the imperial table is plated. It is a tinsel court, unworthy of this authentic Spanish duke, who is soon to rival with the Tsar of all the Russias, Alexander II, at the time, in the words of Castelar, "the greatest potentate on earth."

Part Five

SPLENDOR ON THE STEPPES

XXXIX. THE KEY TO THE PORTFOLIO

Sa physonomie noble e vide annonçait des idées convenables et rares: l'idéal du diplomate . . .

STENDHAL

EVERYTHING seemed to indicate that Russia would soon be willing to resume diplomatic relations with Spain. The almanac of Saint Petersburg for the year 1855, which until then had always spoken only of the "widow of the late king Ferdinand VII," now gave Isabel II the title of Queen. In October 1856 two letters from Alexander II, announcing his succession to the throne, were presented to Queen Isabel by his aide-de-camp, Count Beauckendorff. The Spanish government wished to return the courtesy and considered naming the Duke of Osuna as bearer of the Queen's reply. The next month he was appointed Envoy Extraordinary and Minister Plenipotentiary to the Tsar of all the Russias. Osuna was ill at the time and away from Spain. Nevertheless he accepted, in spite of the cholera epidemic which was raging on the dunes of St. Petersburg, refusing of course, to accept the emolument of $25,000, and the travelling expenses which had been assigned him. The embassy started out for Brussels and was composed of the Duke, his adjutant, Colonel Quiñones, and the young writer, Don Juan Valera, of the diplomatic service.

And Valera, who is certainly free from any suspicion of wishing to flatter Osuna, begins his record of the trip with this jubilant paragraph: "*A Jove principium, Musae, Jovis omnia plena.* Let us begin with the Duke, our providence and our Jove, and say of him that he is the finest person and most generous gentleman I have ever known. We are travelling in princely style. We stop at the best and most fashionable inns, and we have carriages, servants, boxes at the theatre, and everything the heart could desire. The attentions, the consideration and the kindness he lavishes on his adjutant and myself are beyond words."

The first stop was at Brussels where the Beaufort-Spontins rendered homage to Osuna. "They waited attendance upon him and fêted him lavishly where-ever we stopped, and it is plain that his name sounds favourably in the ears of these people of the North, who are greater aristocrats than we, or at least better bred and not so envious. Besides the Duke has an endless number of relatives scattered over Europe, who are proud of the relationship, and with whom he is well pleased, taking pleasure in visiting them and they in entertaining him."

But they had no more than left Brussels when Osuna missed a despatch case containing three letters for St. Petersburg. He grew indignant, flew into a rage, insulted the servant responsible for them for his lack of care, calling him a "dog" and making him go back to Brussels for the case. In Hamm the servant rejoined them. He had not been able to find the case, but he felt greatly insulted. The Duke gave him five hundred francs to mollify him, which he accepted, adding:

"I shall never forgive your Excellency for calling me a dog."

And Valera states: "It is difficult to describe and still more difficult to imagine the Duke's despair over this incident, and above all, his terror lest the same thing should happen with the Royal letters. He has been determined these days, and I do not know if he has changed his mind, to commit suicide if anything happens to the Royal letters."

At Münster they dined with the Princes of Croy-Dülmen and the three unmarried princesses, whom Valera describes as "so many bright, innocent young Cunegundas," and in Berlin with the sovereigns. "The Queen gets Osuna off alone and gives him a sermon on marriage, advising him to take one of the princesses of Croy-Dülmen to wife." And while Valera explains to a fellow-diner how Sancho Panza ate caviar on his island, the King, "a learned fool, most ingenuously pedantic," plies Osuna with questions about "the titles of the house of Osuna, and the history of these titles, about the Virgin of Guadalupe, merino sheep, and heaven only knows what else."

And legend has it, though Valera makes no allusion to it, that as a result of this conversation Osuna had sent from Spain, in a special train, a flock of merinos with shepherds and mastiffs, which he presented to the monarch.

Thirty hours on an impossible railroad to Warsaw. Fourteen degrees below zero. Osuna spent thousands of francs on magnificent beaverskins to keep himself warm. His private secretary, Benjumea, "was so wrapped up in furs and looked so queer that the dogs almost devoured him, taking him for a wild animal from the woods." In Granitza the Duke received a letter from the ruling Prince "by an imperial messenger so beplumed, so radiant in gold braid, so majestic, so huge, and so bewhiskered that I took him for the Emperor himself. . . ." They were lodged in imperial palaces where there was not one single bed, until finally they reached Warsaw, "beautiful but sad like a slave." There they were received in state, accorded every honour, and given an escort. Osuna responded fittingly to these attentions. Fancy the astonishment of those serfs and Cossacks, knowing only the crack of the whip and their meagre ration of raw meat, when Osuna's secretary distributed the following gratuities among them: "In Warsaw, two thousand francs to the servants who accompanied us on the trip; one thousand francs to the messengers; fifteen hundred to the servants who stood guard at our doors; a half rouble for each hour on duty to the soldiers who stood guard in Warsaw for three days."

Over hill and down dale they pursued their way to St. Petersburg. Eight days in covered carriages guided by post boys, dressed in furs from head to foot, riding huge sweating horses, and followed by their luggage, first on wheels and then on sled runners, they crossed the steppes of Russia. Their lanterns were lighted but the glass was frosted over. A grey sky, and white fields, the snow blackened by the wheel-ruts; here and there numb trees stretching their naked shivering arms skyward. At every new hole in the road oaths and lashings for the animals and men who had to pull out conveyances and luggage. The kindly Duke at first protested at such measures, but finally yielded in view of the results they secured. But he compensated them liberally. And in this fashion they reached the banks of the frozen Niemen.

"The Duke, who had worn his uniform all through the trip, in the belief that it was an indispensable requisite," says Valera, "got down from the carriage with me, and unfastening the little box containing the Royal letters, which he never left out of his sight, clasping it to his bosom, like Caesar his Commentaries, crossed the river, holding fast to my arm, and linking my fate to his. . . ."

This was the last time Osuna and Valera were to be

seen arm in arm. There was a profound antagonism between them which was soon to make itself manifest. Osuna was a dazzling horn of plenty, a work of artifice, haughtiness, and ceremony. Valera was "a morsel of life," young, intelligent, impulsive. Besides, he subscribed to the new creed of naturalism, and he regarded Osuna with the lack of comprehension which neo-classicism displayed toward baroque Romanticism. Osuna was fatuous and spectacular, and Valera, in quest of realities, disdained the farce as deceitful. The Russian court seems "churrigueresque" to him, and he makes scornful fun of it. The show seen from behind the wings disgusted him. He did not pay sufficient attention to Osuna. "I forgot to say that the Duke, generous as always . . ." Besides Valera belonged to the petty, impecunious gentry of the provinces, and was really typically middle class. In spite of his liberal ideals he was more conservative than Osuna, all display and adventure, waste and extravagance.

An intelligent, impulsive person like Valera could not make a good diplomat. Pauline Metternich would have said of him, had she seen him, what she said of another: *Il a l'air trop intelligent pour un ambas-*

sadeur; and his difficulties with Osuna came from his being too clever, and from his inability to see him in perspective.

Valera wrote back long letters bubbling over with wit and impertinence with which he made himself not a few enemies in Madrid, Narváez among them. The effect on the Duke was indescribable. Sclafany and Don Antonio Sanz, his agent, wrote him that Valera was making him a laughing-stock with his letters.

The Duke, abetted by Quiñones, who received the same news from his brother in Madrid, blamed Valera for all his little difficulties, and each new contretemps added to the dislike he was acquiring for the secretary.

Valera, heeding his mother's advice, took back what he had said, and showered praises upon the Duke, "extolling him more than Quevedo did his grandfather," but he could not keep the levity out of his tone, nor avoid arousing Osuna's suspicions if matters were not promptly and efficiently attended to in Madrid, if the decorations promised the Slavic dignitaries failed to arrive or if the Spanish government named the former Prime Minister Isturiz to substitute Osuna in his post.

Meanwhile the Duke was received as an ambassador at the Russian Court, and ladies and nobles, headed by the Tsar himself, conspired to keep this generous, lavish Duke in his appointment.

Osuna was satisfied; he had spent millions, but he had not found it necessary to flatter or punish anybody. If his dealings with the great were characterized by impertinence rather than blandishments, in his dealings with his subordinates he was incapable of severity or cruelty. He developed a perfect persecutory mania about Valera, and yet his good breeding was such that the colder he felt toward him the kinder and more delicate he grew in his dealings with him. It reached such a point that Valera himself felt awkward and embarrassed—like Heywood's heroine who is finally smothered by the persistent tenderness of her vengeful spouse.

XL. THE TSAR OF ALL THE RUSSIAS

Eternel ennemi des suprêmes puissances.
RACINE

RESPLENDENT as the sun," was the Duke as he went to present the royal missives. Two huge mitred chamberlains preceded him, from whose lofty tiaras descended cascades of ostrich plumes. The master of ceremonies walked beside him. Quiñones and Valera in uniform were accompanied by other dignitaries. They traversed salons, drawing-rooms, large and small, each richer, more ornate and more golden than the other. On either side, cassocks and green liveries, embroidered with eagles, formed an aisle. Quiñones counted the number of steps: four hundred and fifty-seven in a straight line. Negro slaves in gold turbans threw open the doors of each new room. And finally, like a figure on an altarpiece, Alexander II, in all his glory. The Duke, somewhat confused, made his speech, to which the Tsar replied briefly and in a low voice. This man with the mutton-chop whiskers, and hard, blue, frozen eyes—"a ferocious sheep," his teacher, Joukovski, called him, was wearing a uniform, and a white cloak embossed with ornaments of gold braid, crosses, chains, and with bindings of blue Siberian fox. His boots were high, of fine leather, like a lion tamer's, and his embroidered trousers were a pale blue. One hand held a curved sword and the other, his white-plumed helmet. This was the Tsar, the tender-hearted merciless Tsar, who let a marvellous Empress grieve herself to death to lay the throne at the feet of Princess Dolgouruki. This was the Tsar, the All-Mighty, the Lord's Anointed, the Generalissimo, the Pontifex Maximus. His absolute sovereignty was recognized and proclaimed as the first article of the laws of his empire of the steppes: the Emperor of all the Russias is an autocratic monarch whose power is unlimited. God Himself orders his supreme power to be obeyed, not only out of fear, but from the dictates of conscience.

An imperial order—a *Ukase*—could countermand prevailing laws, and its command was imposed with this flawless reasoning: "If you do not obey the law, you disobey the Tsar who has issued it; if you oppose the Tsar, you are opposing God who has designated him: so hands to the back, a gag in the mouth, and the knout."

The reprisals of the "Iron Tsar" were still in practice. Communication with foreign countries was prohibited; studies were limited to certain subjects, and that of philosophy forbidden. The word "liberty" was banned as being revolutionary, and "if the owner of a dog named Tyrant was so unfortunate as to lose him," says one historian, "he could not advertise for him in the papers except by the name of Faithful."

The Crimean War made a breach in this despotic attitude, and the first rays of light began to filter through. After that mysterious Alexander I, the autocracy changed, "and its undisputed power seems to find barriers, and the term of its grandeur can be glimpsed." The time will soon come when the nobles will say: "Until the Emancipation Proclamation we never kept accounts and we drank champagne; since the Emancipation, we keep accounts and drink beer." And nobody is so poor as the rich man—memory makes misers of us—who keeps accounts.

The revolutionists penetrated to Tzarkoiselo with their proclamations. *The Bell* was to be seen on the royal reading-table; the Tzarina Maria Alexandrovna wept over a letter of Hertzen's. Hertzen never weakened in his campaign which began with the publication in 1845 of his novel *Whose Fault Is It?* which deals with the problem of a man in love with a woman whom the laws of society have bound to another. (Eighty years later Gladkow was to present the obverse side of the conflict: the exclusiveness which every true love demands, and with which the revolution had not reckoned.)

The word *nihilism* made its appearance about this time (1855), and Dostoiewsky returned from the *House of the Dead*. It was he who said: "Nihilism has developed among us because we are all nihilists."

And as a matter of fact "nihilism is much closer to the palace of the tzars than to the hovels of the peasants," to use Castelar's phrase: the Grand Duchess Elena Pavlovna, a favourite with the Emperor, encouraged liberalism in her salons, and the Empress Marie Alexandrovna herself actively worked for the emancipation, as the revolutionary Prince Kropotkin sets forth in his memoirs. Kropotkin had been one of the Tzar's pages since 1857, and lived in the court. Tolstoy, too, was an officer in the army.

The Tolstoy whom Osuna knew in St. Petersburg was not Count Leo, but a general attached to the Ministry of Foreign Affairs. It is probable that these two prodigies never met. Leo Tolstoy was not yet thirty: he wore the uniform and lived in grand style, but his rebellious spirit showed itself in certain dandyish characteristics, in a certain haughty impertinence. His first visit to Paris was in 1857, where he watched and learned, keeping aloof from society and literature. From there he went to Lucerne. He stayed at the Schweizerhof with other aristocrats, idlers like himself. One day a street-singer intones his song beneath the terrace. The guests listen complacently, but when he passes his hat, nobody gives him anything. Thereupon Leo Tolstoy has him come up and drink with him at his table, to the speechless indignation of the astounded guests.

Meanwhile the court heaps attentions on Osuna, in homage to him, rather than to what he represents. At a banquet of eighty officers which the Emperor gave in his honour the day he presented the Royal letters he made the acquaintance of the Grand Duke

Constantine, who was seated at his right, and of Orloff, Gortchakoff, Nesselrode, and other outstanding figures who were later to become his friends. On the fifteenth of December he dined beside the beautiful Empress at Tzarkoiselo. And he was never to forget those fathomless black eyes.

In a short time Osuna was the pet of the Russian court. The high officials presented him with maps, lacquered bibelots, uniforms, and a collection of oriental coins and medals which will later occupy nine cabinets in his numismatic collection. They felt obliged to return the favours of the Duke whose attentions never ceased. One New Year's day, in recollection of his ancestor, the Grand Duke of Osuna, he sent magnificent antique fans to the ladies of the court and the diplomatic corps; exquisite flowers were a daily affair. The Tzar had only to voice a desire and Osuna satisfied it at once. Special trains brought a bear-hunter from Asturias, a pack of beagles, a kennel of hounds, etc.

Alexander II honoured him; in a *Ukase* of December 22, 1857, he conferred the Grand Cross of St. Alexander Newski upon him, "set with diamonds and as a token of his personal friendship"—runs the diploma—and afterwards the coveted chain of St. Andrew, crucified saltirewise.

The Tsar accorded him ambassadorial rank, second only to the French Ambassador, although he was not given this category in Spain until 1860, and he showered him with honours and gifts; one day, an enormous stuffed bear; years later a life-size portrait of himself, by Aabpoba, with this inscription: "To the Duke of Osuna and the Infantado, Prince of Éboli and Squilache" (1860).

In a land of princes, Osuna made much of his titles. He was not to be left behind. "The Russians are exaggerated in everything," said Valera. Theirs was the kingdom of the superlative, the empire of the unbounded: the biggest cannon, the thickest bell, etc. Where could Osuna have found a better stage than this, for his pompous, vain realities. Even the court of the Tsars was astonished at his blinding display. *Le dandisme est le dernier éclat d'heroïsme dans les decadences*, wrote a dandy.

Fragments of this aggressive Spanish meteor, which crashed to earth with a deafening clatter of gold and diamonds, reached the throne. The homage of the true dandy takes the form of an impertinence which stakes everything, and which, under a bored, disdainful exterior may hide a consuming passion, capable of wounding the thing it most loves.

When Osuna reached Russia, he came to bend his knee before this Tsar with the staring eyes, the most powerful man on earth, the despot who was the master of his subjects' lives and possessions, but who was not master of himself, for on his wrists he wore golden fetters—a sign, as Paleologue wrote, that *Il avait toujours éprouvé pour les femmes un irrésistible attrait.* The Tsarina was dying of jealousy and loneliness; a marvellous woman, bowed down by illness, woe and necklaces of pearls. Nothing could calm her fever, however much she swathed herself in astrakhan or chinchilla or beaver or sables. Nobody had such beautiful furs nor such beseeching, tortured eyes.

One day everybody was talking about a blue fox which had recently been discovered in a remote corner of Siberia. It was rare and very hard to capture. Its silky and unusual fur made it a coveted prize. The Tsar wanted to secure all there were and sent out a costly expedition of the most skilful hunters. After some time and considerable efforts they returned with enough skins so the imperial furrier could fashion a small cape of them. The Tsar presented it to the Tsarina. And while all the court admired the unique stole in which the lovely empress wrapped her feverish shoulders, the Duke of Osuna sent, at his own expense, a similar expedition to Siberia, and when it returned he had jackets of the same skins made for his coachman and his footman.

XLI. AT THE SIGN OF THE TWO-HEADED EAGLE

Ce ne sont qu'uniformes plastronés d'or, épaulettes étoilées de diamants, brochettes de décorations, plaques d'émaux et de pierreries formant sur les poitrines des foyers de lumière.

THÉO. GAUTIER

WHEN the Duke of Osuna, muffled in furs and armed to the teeth goes out with the Emperor to hunt bears, wolves, and wild boars, everything about the expedition is real: the Tsar is a tsar, the Duke is a duke, the furs are furs, the bear is a bear, and the cold, the dangers and the sufferings are authentic. And yet, it reminds one of a scene from a bad operetta. Why? Perhaps it is the epoch. Perhaps it is the place, the perspective.

Nevertheless, in no other part of the world is there more real or substantial luxury than in Russia. The palaces are of marble, jasper, porphyry, and malachite, and the vases and statues of gold. At soirées or dances, the mistress of the house sometimes goes so far as to display in glass cases or jewel boxes, carefully guarded, the jewels she is unable to wear. There glittered the diamonds which were wrenched from the mountains of the Ural by slaves who work naked winter and summer so they can secrete nothing.

In the imperial chambers the golden exuberance goes to unheard-of lengths. The portraits of former emperors are displayed on a kind of altar. The footmen wear the green and gold imperial eagle embroidered on the seams of their garments. And yet everything has the air of a gigantic spectacle whose effects have been achieved by skilful stage decoration. And when the Duke of Osuna, in his general's uniform, sits for hours and hours on horseback, with the temperature eighteen degrees below zero, accompanying the Tsar at a review of the troops, or when, as Ambassador with military rank, he proceeds to the *razwood,* followed by Colonel Quiñones and escorted by the Don Cossacks, or when he goes to Kronstadt and drives about in his magnificent sleigh among the warships held prisoners in the ice, with the fortress' six thousand cannon looming above them, Osuna loses his own reality and turns into a perfect comedian.

And the same was true of other of the ambassadors who vied with each other in luxurious display: Lord Granville, Count Esterhazy, and, above all, Count Morny, who up to the time of Osuna's advent, had been "the most magnificent of all the ambassadors." Morny was the dean of the corps; he represented a nation which demanded the highest honours for him, and put extraordinary resources at his command. He had a brilliant suite: dukes, counts, carriages, liveried servants, and even a private collection of works of art.

A few months later Osuna burst upon the scene. Quiñones and Valera constituted his whole staff. He did not receive a cent from his country, not even the title or rank of ambassador, which was soon conferred upon him by the Tsar. Yet through his own efforts and his personal prestige he triumphed immediately. And he was not, like Morny, a man of great talent. Nor even a shrewd diplomat. He was only a Spanish gentleman whose sole purpose in life was to be just that.

In his rivalry with Morny the contrast between them was striking. Morny hated everything exaggerated. Morny was a lover of the classic. When he went to excess, it was for the sake of some advantage to be gained. His luxury was that of the practical politician, who regards extravagance or munificence as adjuncts to success. But not Osuna. Osuna was a romantic, a lost star flying through space. He squandered and spent, left and right, but without any purpose, for he was the purpose. Excessive, lavish, impertinent, he triumphed because of the admiration he inspired, but never through premeditated calculations. At his side "Morny reeks of parvenu a mile off," says Valera. There is a detail that bears this out. Morny had not yet received the title of Duke, nor had his paternal arms quartered with the imperial, and when he reaches Russia he improvises a coat of arms for his carriages served by footmen in white, red, and gold liveries, scandalously allusive to the maternity of Queen Hortense: a hortensia in the centre of the shield and this motto: *Tace sed memento* (Be silent but remember).

A peculiar way of being silent. A recent authority on heraldry holds the theory that an emblem engraved on an escutcheon has never been aught but a trade mark, used to advertise the excellence and universality of a certain company.

XLII. LEGENDS OF THE NEVA

Le cuisinier plume les oies
Ah! tombe, neige,
Tombe, et que n'ai-je
Ma bien-aimée entre mes bras.
APOLLINAIRE

THE palace Don Quixote saw in the cave of Montesinos must have been on the order of this," wrote Valera describing the one in which the Duke of Osuna established himself with his secretaries and "servants who are so many other Dukes." It was a magnificent building, imposing in appearance, with striped sentry-boxes on the deep hard-packed snow. It was situated opposite the Nicolai bridge, on the famous dike that separated the river from the dingy city which the knout had built over the mud of the dunes. When they were not frozen the blessed waters of the Neva, a dull milky white in colour, flowed past the front of the palace. The interior was dazzling with its profusion of gilt, mirrors, and glass arches which adorned the drawing-rooms, and its conservatory with an illuminated fountain, and grottoes overgrown with ivy, flowers, tropical plants, bushes, and vines; everywhere there was an agreeable even temperature, thanks to the many fires. At the great dinners which the Duke gave for Prince and Princess Dolgouruki, Orloff, Galatzine, Gortchakoff, Count Adlerberg, Morny, Esterhazy, Lord Wodehouse, and the most beautiful ladies of the court, the famous sterlet soup was served "which costs over one thousand silver roubles a plate," and fruits from America on the plant where they grew, which, like the flowers from Valencia and Nice for the ladies, arrived in special heated trains. One historian said: "He astonishes the Cossacks with entertainments like those of the Arabian Nights," and it is said that at one of them, after dinner, he threw the gold dinner service into the depths of the Neva, to the astonishment of several dozen guests.

It is doubtful that this took place; but what is certain is that, unlike the *dux mercader*, Osuna did not have nets prepared to catch his treasures in order to secretly rescue them afterwards. When Osuna threw his dishes into the sea it was to lose them for good, like Alcibiades, and all that remained of the gesture were the eyes wide with admiration above the surface of the water.

Osuna does not rescue his treasures because he cannot speculate with them. He was unbelievably lavish and extravagant. "There is not a soul who does not take advantage of him, nor a rogue who is not generous, and even lavish, at his expense," says Valera, and by way of example: "The Duke has already spent over a thousand dollars in the collection of photographs he has had taken."

But the Duke was not a philanthropist. *La charité, dit Dieu, ça ne m' étonne pas,* a convert, Péguy, has written. Charity requires humility and self-effacement: to give the alms, and let no one perceive the hand from which it fell. And Osuna was incapable of effacing himself. He had an excess of pride and a lack of humility and the Christian spirit.

Neither was he intelligent nor shrewd. He let himself be exploited by friends, women, and agents. Since he was unwilling to commit a deception he had to be deceived. He must have always behaved better than the others, been unwilling to take advantage or beguile. It was his business to forgive; for this he was magnanimous and noble; his loftiness prevented his being aware of the existence of low trickery. His "anæmia of the will" did not interfere with the vigour he displayed in securing respect for anyone under his protection, "for even if I could overlook a slight to myself, I could never tolerate the least offense to a person in whom I have placed my trust," he wrote on a certain occasion to Bravo Murillo. Impertinent with the great, haughty to his rivals, Osuna could always be won over by those who needed him: by those he considered his inferiors, and there were so many of them.

Je trouve que la Russie est encore superbe dans son comte Orloff, said the Countess Damrémont. Despite the fact that he was a veteran of the Napoleonic Wars, Count, afterwards Prince, Orloff was still a diplomat of splendid presence and martial bearing. When he went to Paris in the winter of 1856 he caused a sensation with his gold-embroidered green tunic, and the diamond-set miniatures of Nicholas I and Alexander II which he wore on his breast. Naples has its Vesuvius, Madrid, the gleaming banner of its Osuna, and Russia, its Orloff, the pride of her plenipotentiaries. But

Orloff was even more respected for his magnificent breed of mares than for his diplomatic achievements. The origin of the Orloff stock goes back to the eighteenth century; it is also known as Rissah, and was obtained by Count Alexander Orloff by crossing Arabian and Danish horses, some of which, Eclipse, Dedalus or Tartar, cost him as high as twelve thousand dollars. Barss I was the sire of this breed, which was characterized by its delicate head, broad chest, deerlike neck, pointed ears, thin, sloping flanks and slender, arched tail. This is the breed of trotters which in sleigh races can do four kilometres in seven minutes, "the greatest known equine velocity."

The breed was extended throughout all Russia, but Count Orloff had the best specimens. And Osuna suddenly took a fancy to the most highly prized of them all, the favourite of Slavic connoisseurs of horseflesh, and the pride of Orloff's stable. Its owner refused to sell at any price. Osuna raised his offer. Orloff rejected them all; but during his absence, the Countess made the sale. On the Count's return he asked for his horse. But it was no longer in the stable. It had passed to Osuna's, wearing its red patent leather collar trimmed with golden bells about its long, jet-black throat. Orloff called on the Duke and attempted to void the sale.

"I'm sorry," said Osuna, "but the horse is in use." And stepping to the window he pointed him out to his former owner, turning a water-wheel, his mane and tail shorn away.

His own horses were shod "with silver shoes and diamond nails," according to the popular fancy, which wove a fairy tale out of the humble fact that horses' shoes are fastened on with nails that have diamond-shaped heads.

It is also told of the Duke of Richelieu that, when he entered Vienna the horses of his cortege were shod with silver, and it is also said that the shoes were lightly fastened on so they came off easily, causing great excitement and commotion in the spectators, for each person was anxious to secure such a valuable good-luck symbol.

But Richelieu was not generous. He was an ostentatious miser, an evil angel who robbed and exploited in order to make a show afterwards. For this reason it pleased him to establish his credit with this ringing trail of silver. In spite of the fact that Osuna is nearer to us, his gesture is more doubtful and legendary, for

Don Mariano Téllez-Girón, Twelfth Duke of Osuna, during his Embassy in Russia

the horseshoes he paid for were not intended for the street hordes, but for his horses, and were tightly nailed on; as the horses trotted briskly along they were hardly visible. This Spanish nobleman was not trying to awaken noisy acclamations with his silver.

Like the Spanish knight he was, Osuna shattered more than one lance on the Slavic steppes. One day he went to the palace. Quiñones was accompanying him. They did not wait for Valera, who was never on time. This day they were more Spaniards than diplomats: they were going to be late. In the open sleigh Osuna protected himself against the biting wind with a magnificent ermine cape, covered with crosses and decorations, on which the cold and the sun impinged as on the smooth hard surface of the frozen Neva. They reached the Winter Palace. The Tsar was seated on his throne surrounded by the diplomatic corps. It was a closed session, and had already begun. Osuna slipped in, silent and irritated. The Grandee of the Grandees could find no chair, so, unfastening his ermine cape he rolled it up and used it for a seat. When the meeting was over, as they were leaving, an attendant came after him with the jewelled cape he had left on the floor. Osuna waved him aside saying that the ambassadors of Spain were not in the habit of carrying away their chairs.

A cavalier's cape, which covers, protects and intimately lives with him is of no use if it has been turned to some lowly purpose, if it has been humiliated. Legendary in everything, in all his acts Osuna emphasizes the mythical, the traditional. Gómez Ocerín has traced the origin of this anecdote. Some make it go back as far as the Crusades. There are versions of this story in Timoneda, in Lope de Vega, and even in Cervantes who wrote in his *Viaje al Parnaso:*

Mas si quieres salir de tu querella
alegre y no confuso, y consolado,
dobla tu capa y siéntate sobre ella.

All these stories reached Madrid in different versions, some contradictory, others incomplete, and the popular echo, mixing them all together, forged a legend of them. There in distant Russia the powerful house of Girón was crumbling to pieces just as the hard surface of the Neva splits up when the spring thaws set in. The waters rise and carry the ice-floes downstream. On a certain day a golden, festooned barge appears on the waters. In it rides the governor of St. Petersburg, carrying out an annual rite: he fills a goblet with the melting water, and presents it to the Tsar who returns it to the city brimming over with gold.

XLIII. DIPLOMACY IN CRINOLINES

Corps diplomatique composé d'âmes subtiles, étherées et feminines. . . . La diplomatie en crinoline vaut tout autant au moins que celle du paletot.

FRANZ LISZT

THE Empress Eugénie was more than right when she exclaimed on receiving the news of the Crimean War:

"This is the work of that embassy of women."

It was the Princess Lieven, with her imposing aspect, "dignity without beauty," who countermanded the Emperor's orders, and decided the war on the basis of her information. She was a secret agent of the Russian chancellor, Nesselrode, as was the beautiful Maria Kalergis, of whom Gautier said:

Sphinx enterré par l'avalanche,
Gardien des glaciers étoilés,
Et qui sous sa poitrine blanche
Cache des blancs secrets gelés.

And hiding place sometimes of sinister designs. Lesser luminaries of this "diplomatic corps in crinoline" were the Princess Bagration, Madame Swetchine, and perhaps, a little later, Sophie Troubetskoi, who conspired in favour of the Spanish king. "Ethereal, subtle souls," as Liszt called them; souls of Russian women "artificially lighted by the gas of the present-day feminism." With Alexander II, the Tsar of the fettered wrists, Gortchakoff entered as chancellor, and dispersed these beguiling crinolines, rejecting their services. And this took place the same year that Osuna reached Russia, so he was saved by a happy chance from being wooed to disaster by these sirens.

But there was no dearth of others, attracted more by his pocketbook than by his despatch case. "The Duke has brought with him and has shown to many of the ladies an album of photographs of the gardens of the Alameda, his palace at Guadalajara, and other castles. The young ladies, especially the maids of honour, open up eyes like saucers at the sight of these 'castles in Spain.' He dangles this bait, and he struts, and preens himself and attitudinizes; he says he wants to get married and then it surprises him that the young women get into a flutter over him, and affecting despair, he calls himself the unhappiest gentleman that ever lived, for there is not a maiden who is not ready to sacrifice her maidenhood in his arms." But Osuna was more of a Don Quixote than a Don Juan; the human passions in him were subordinate to those of the dandy. Lovelace, the darling of the ladies, wrote to his beloved Lucasta, on going to the wars: "I could not love thee dear so much, loved I not honour more."

Osuna was extraordinarily satisfied in Russia. He prolonged his mission and complacently viewed the intrigues carried on to keep him from being replaced. This huge figurehead had found his proper setting. Osuna was like the man whom Larra described, "who spends the morning paying visits and leaving cards from door to door." Paying calls, says Valera, was the Duke's perennial occupation. "He is tireless, and I don't understand how he does not drop from sheer fatigue. He neither sleeps nor rests. He dresses and undresses six or seven times a day, and there is never an entertainment at which he is not present, nor a person on whom he does not call. With this and his exquisite manners and his long rigamarole of titles he has captivated the Russians. Last night he came home about three or four o'clock in the morning, and at seven or eight he was ready to go bear-hunting with the Emperor."

Heralded by magnificent camellias, he visited the beauties in their cushioned boudoirs and the actresses in their dressing-rooms.

Like a sun Osuna moved among the major planets: the beautiful Princess Korsakoff, who caused a sensation in Europe with her exotic features and her bizarre attire; Princess Matilde, who swiftly traversed the Russian court on the arm of the opulent and savage Demidoff; Princess Lucia Dolgoruky (the other Dolgoruky, Catherine, was still a child and unknown; but a little later she was to win the Emperor's heart); Princess Youssoupoff, who dined to the music of an orchestra of thirty musicians and the plashing of fountains; and, the favourite of all, the granddaughter of the great Souvarov Italianiski, the little princess Souvarov, whom the Duke was on the point of marrying. "His Excellency is completely smitten. He always dances the first quadrille with her and sends her the most beautiful flowers," testifies Valera. "The princess deserves it all. She is at the age of perfection. . . . She joins the sweetness and gentleness of the dove to the cunning of the serpent." A little later he was on the point of marrying Princess Radziwill, who was forgotten for the Andalusian charms of a daughter of the Marchioness of Campo Alange, although he did not marry her either.

From the moment he reached Russia Osuna drew the ladies to him. "The beautiful Helena Strattmann would make him her Menelaus," wrote Valera, and at any event she makes him prolong his mission indefinitely. "A Calmuck beauty" brings him into rivalry with the minister, General Tolstoy, and he comes off the victor. The amazing beauty of this woman almost caused Valera to break his neck on one occasion.

But ordinarily Valera kept better watch on his step. Behind the scenes of the glittering stage, the eye that watched carefully, *en coulisse,* might discover rivalries and difficulties. Valera, who made fun of the Duke because of his amusing adventures with Mlle. de Théric, of the French Theatre, lost his own heart to another actress in the same company, the beautiful Brohan. Madeleine Brohan was a member of the Comédie Française; she was twenty-four years old, married but separated from the poet Uchard, and she was acting in Russia, where she was "surrounded by gallants who made the theater echo with applause," and buried her feet in their flowers. She was wooed by the most prominent members of the diplomatic corps, Prince Orloff, the Marquis of Oldoini, the father of the famous Countess Castigilione, and the Duke of Osuna "who visits her assidiously and writes her tender billets-doux," and sends her bouquets of camellias with his majordomo, a very learned German who devotes his leisure moments to literature.

Valera's correspondence gives details of this passion which was shared by the ambassador and his secretary, whose relations with Madeleine "were like those of the Jew and the Inquisitor of Lisbon with Cunegunda. He goes at one hour and I at another, and we never meet." But though they did not meet, they were suspicious of each other, and this fomented the bad feeling between them to such a point that at the hour fixed for Valera to take his leave of him, Osuna went out driving in an open carriage with Quiñones.

Barbey was quite correct in saying that the dandy's way of pleasing a woman was to treat her badly, Madeleine Brohan—like all the women with classic profile and smoothly parted hair who played a part in Osuna's life: Eugenia Montijo or Lady Villiers, Mlle. Théric or Princess Leonor of Salm-Salm—was a repetition of the one type of woman who always appears in the life and love of the dandy: the unfeeling, rapacious, ruthless woman whom Baudelaire, the intellectual of the dandies, defined as: *Statue aux yeux de jais—Grande ange au front d'airain.*

If Madeleine Brohan was a diamond that cut and buried herself in Osuna's breast, like the others, to Valera she was the muse that tormented and finally inspired the poet in him, and he sang of her in *Saudades,* calling her Elisena:

Cuando la cándida nieve
En densos copos caía.

* * * * *

Yo robaba de tu boca
La canción aun no nacida.

Part Six

THE SMOKE OF OSUNA

XLIV. ENNUI AT BEAURAING

Je ne trouve partout que lâche flatterie, qu' injustice,
intérêt, trahison, fourberie . . . et je hais tous les hommes.
MOLIÈRE

In a way, Osuna was ahead of his day. As he had a gift for languages, rare at the time, and spoke a number of them like his native tongue, he possessed an unusual capacity for ubiquity, which contributed to the somewhat fabulous conception of him that existed in Spain. He came and went from Russia, London, and Vienna. One day he was in Madrid and the next in St. Petersburg. And the following incident took place in one of these trips in the year '58: they were a long way from St. Petersburg and the secretaries of the embassy, Diosdado and the Marquis of Villar who were in one carriage, caught up with that of the Duke which had stopped. When they inquired as to the reasons for the halt, the Duke told them it was impossible for him to go on with the trip because his servant was wearing a cap that did not match his suit. They tried to placate him; all in vain. The trip was interrupted while Diosdado returned to St. Petersburg in search of a proper cap.

In the spring of 1861 he left the Russian court and in the autumn attended the coronation of Wilhelm I, and his consecration in Königsberg. His display and lavishness were so astounding that the King of Prussia, wishing to fittingly honour him, created the diamond collar of the Order of the Red Eagle expressly for him and named him the first chevalier of the new order.

On his travels through Europe he enjoyed the prestige which the friendship of the Tsars then gave. When it snowed in Paris, Osuna crossed the Champs Élysées swathed in furs and driving a magnificent sleigh in the style of the *troika,* with the horses' heads arched outwards, and glittering sleigh bells. But his passage was only a flash, a dazzling reverberation on the snow. He went alone, always alone. Nowhere did he find the companion soul for his own. Perhaps the one which most resembled his was that of the beautiful woman, proud and legendary like himself, and who also inspired dislike, whom he often saw at the court of the Tuileries. But neither he nor she was aware of each other: the invisible mirror which every dandy has before his eyes day and night prevented them from seeing one another. This woman was La Castiglione, who left this phrase, characteristic of her style and ideas, in her correspondence: *Je suis moi et m'en contente ne voulant rien être par les autres et pour les autres. Seulement je reconnais que je ne parais pas bonne à cause de mon caractère fier, franc et libre, qui me fait être en tout et pour tous, carrée, crue et dure. De sorte qu'on me déteste, mais ça m'est égal. Je ne tiens pas même à plaire.*

Osuna made no effort to please either, in spite of the fact that he was a comedian who fed his vanity on the public's applause, and who could not do without glory —a crown, like that of Christine of Sweden's, which he neither needed nor did it suffice.

He paid repeated visits to London, the court of silence. He bought a thoroughbred from Tilbury, acquired a new style of landau, a brake. He divided his favours among the fashionable beauties: the hazel-eyed, black-haired Duchess of Wellington, and the blondes: Lady Jocelyn, Lady Craven, the Countess of Clarendon. It is said that he was greatly attracted by the little Marchioness of Chandos; but suddenly he fell in love with a beautiful young thing he had met at the gatherings of the aristocratic Countess of Jersey. The damsel was the daughter of the Countess, Clementina Villiers. As discreet as she was beautiful, she fired Osuna's ardour by rejecting his suit. To those who, in their astonishment, failed to understand Clementina's reasons for refusing her hand to Osuna, she replied that the Duke bored her insufferably for "he paid visits that lasted three or four hours without saying a single thing that was amusing." Don Juan Valera had also found Osuna tedious in extreme, but nobody before Clementina Villiers had stated the case in such grave terms. Osuna, who had always shied at marriage, bore her no ill will. He even kept, and in duplicate, an engraving by Robinson of a portrait of Lady Clementina as Undine, as well as one of the Countess of Jersey with Lady Angela Villiers, engraved by Lewis.

But his pride was wounded. For the first time in his life Osuna saw things a little clearly. He was interested in finding out if he was ruined. No, the accounts of his holdings and possessions showed a balance of

232,057,312 reales (over $10,000,000). He began to suspect that his pomp was but a snare and a delusion. And then came surfeit, spleen, sombre neurasthenia, and his misanthropy reached the point of wanting to flee even from himself:

. . . la grotesque ballade
Ne distrait plus le front de ce cruel malade.

And he buried himself in Beauraing, the magnificent estate which, as Count of Beaufort, he possessed in Belgium.

It was not that he felt boredom; he lacked the adequate organ for this, and the habit. Thus, when he settled down behind the turrets of Beauraing, what he did was to absent himself from his own depression, and he ordered things to go on in his other palaces just as though he were there. But he was not at ease in Beauraing, though he lived there, in retirement and solitude, like "an original."

From the year '63, when he ascended to the rank of Lieutenant-General, he possessed every class of distinctions and honours. He was a worthy representative of his house. He had done everything *comme il faut*. He could now retire, satisfied but disillusioned. His pride made defeat unthinkable; he must not weaken, even in his own eyes, and he felt so lonely; the loneliness of the person who cannot admit his failures, and lives as a stranger to himself.

He shuts himself up in the carpeted rooms of his palace, amidst his silk-covered furniture, with its fringes, its rosettes, and its hangings, porcelains, and portraits. A faint light falls from the cut glass chandeliers. And the Duke walks over to the fireplace and stirs the embers with the wrought silver tongs, or strolls to the window and drums upon the panes.

It rains day after day. The cloud-hooded mountains send rain and gloom down the windows. The gravel walks of the broad avenues glisten; a black snail leaves its trail across the path; the magnolias, with their half-open bodices, droop plaintively, and against the wall a drenched clump of hydrangeas shakes itself from side to side like a rebellious child evading the sponge.

Osuna's blond locks are turning grey, like the pointed reddish moustache. His nearsightedness throws a veil across the distant blurred horizon. He feels cut off and imprisoned, like the flower enclosed in the glass paperweight.

But one day he shakes off his neurasthenia, leaves the walls of his castle, and sets out, determined to marry: *Si*—as he says in a letter—*j'en trouve qui veuille de moi.*

XLV. THE BLUE FLAME

Avalanche, veux-tu m'emporter dans ta chute?
BAUDELAIRE

OSUNA promenaded his neurasthenia and his incipient gout about the smart watering places of the day. "Baden sets the pace for Europe," because Osuna and the other fashionables go there. And in Baden, Europe's summer capital, he punctiliously performed the whole series of rites to which the invalid must submit if he is a person of fashion. The author of the *Manuel du Fashionable* was right in saying that in those days "taking the waters is a source of constant exertion." And in Baden Osuna listened to the concerts in the "Conversation Room," or trailed his ennui in a "Doble Daumont," to La Favorita, a charming eighteenth-century villa, crowned by two thick counterpoised 'scutcheons.

He made the round of other watering places, Spa, Aix, Wiesbaden. In Wiesbaden he rode on horse-back down the avenue of plane-trees, as far as the pillars of the Roman baths, or to Platte Castle, guarded by two carved deer at its park gate. On these drives he passed lovely Amazons, who as they rode by measured him with their steady glance.

It was the heyday of equestrian prowess. Paris was in a decline; St. Petersburg was a hotbed of revolutionary activities. Vienna was the most aristocratic court of the day. There the Empress imposed her silhouette, her manners, and her styles. She belonged to the house of Louis of Bavaria, and the face of this marvellous Elizabeth of Austria bore the stamp of genius and wilfulness. With her "Calmuck face," her swan's neck, and her body like a palm-tree, she galloped at breakneck speed through the dense forests of Gôdôllô, followed by Esterhazy and the other Magyar nobles. She banished the old-fashioned hoop skirt from the court, and introduced the tightly clasped waist and the two-yard train which flattered her slenderness. After her, swaying their ruffled skirts in waltz rhythm, came the most beautiful princesses, the Princess of Lichtenstein or Lobkowitz, Metternich or Anersperg, Schwarzenberg or Windischgraetz . . . and, above all, the Princesses of Salm-Salm, the flower of the Prater.

And it was an Amazon of the house of Salm-Salm who conquered Osuna, tamed his rebelliousness and put him through the hoop. She belonged to a generation of whip-lashes, women with an air of fragility and a soul of stone; flexible, insinuating women, but with a heart encased in whalebone and energetic in their decisions. Whips with long, billowing trains, who, once in the saddle, stop at no obstacle.

Her Serene Highness Maria Leonor Crescencia Catherine of Salm-Salm, princess of Salm-Salm and of the Holy Roman Empire, was twenty-eight years younger than the Duke of Osuna when he obtained the Royal permission to marry on January 29, 1866. She was born in Frankfort on January 21, 1842, the only daughter of Prince Franz Joseph Frederick and Maria Josephine, born Princess Lowenstein-Wertheim-Rosemberg.

Among the Duke's gifts to the bride was the ribbon of the Noble Ladies of the Order of Maria Luisa, conceded in Madrid on February 6. At last the Duke of Osuna was marrying—in Wiesbaden on the fourth of April—a beautiful twenty-four-year-old princess of one of the oldest houses in Europe: the house of the ruling princes of Salm-Salm, whose feudal castle was located in Anholt, and who were Princes of Ahans, Bocholt, Anholt, Dukes of Hoogstraten, etc., and whose arms bear two hauriant fish on a field of gules.

A blue flame, in her azure brocades, with a long train adorned with ruffles, loops and ruchings, the Princess Leonor has the high forehead, the sculptured profile, the steely eyes, the smooth, fine skin and glacial expression *de ces bouches sans lèvres* that Baudelaire loved. Her hair covers her shoulders with a cascade of thick golden curls. Her sullen beauty so conceals the perfidiousness of her expression that one might imagine her, like Barbey's *Haute Claire,* to have fallen from Heaven.

But she quickly gets to her feet. A blue flame, at once fiery and cold, precise and flexible, a flaming sword that seeks a victim, she was able to ensnare Osuna, make him wholly hers, and without loving him, without wanting love, link herself to his destruction until she becomes the torch which sets off the pyre.

Osuna solicited indefinite leave to reside abroad, and he took his love to Beauraing.

> *Ayons un alcôve à trumeaux*
> *Ayons un lit à bergerade.*

The Princess Leonor paid her first visit to Spain about the middle of August. Her sister, the Countess of Salm-Salm, came with her. The new Duchess of Osuna caused a sensation at the court. The Dowager Countess of Montijo gave an exquisite fête in her honour at her country place in Carabanchel. Merimée met her the year of her marriage and wrote to the Countess of Montijo that he had seen the Duchess of Osuna, "*assez belle personne et qui a l'air de porter la culotte, comme on dit.*"

The Princess-Duchess of Osuna was "not only one of the highest-born ladies in the North of Europe, belonging as she did to the oldest German aristocracy, but she was a classic type of Northern beauty." Another exotic novelty with which Osuna surprised Madrid. Her haughty enigmatic air aroused so much wonderment "that some supposed she was the bearer of a special mission, in support of Queen Isabel, from the Emperors of Russia and Austria and the King of Prussia."

The idyll of this *grande taciturne* and the neurasthenic Duke was of brief duration. The blue flame swells, rises, and guides the brave craft on to the rocks. She brings to Osuna's irreproachable integrity the demoralization of the petty German courts ruled over by dancers and actresses. The Princess-Duchess covers herself with jewels, raises the rents, grinds down the tenants, travels, runs into debt, and spends recklessly. All that remains of her visit at Beauraing is a portrait of her by Marcos Hiráldez Acosta.

Osuna had no attraction for Princess Leonor. What did draw her, though, was the vertigo of his abyss. And she made for it, bold and determined. The runaway steed of the Giróns at last had its Amazon, its Valkyrie, who was to ride it to a fall. On it dashes, a broken garland of roses for a bit, and on its back the flame of an imperious woman who spurs it on with the fury of a lost soul.

XLVI. AT THE MERCY OF THE GALE

Quand un grave marin voit que le vent l'emporte
Et que les mâts brisés pendant tous sur le pont,
Que dans son grand duel la mer est la plus forte
* * * * *
Il se croise les bras dans un calme profond.
A. de Vigny

THE mighty galleon of the Osuna has set out to sea, laden with treasure. Its sails are unfurled to the wind. On its ensign, the motto "Better to fly." It goes to "brave the perils and fortunes of the deep."

When the tempest rocks the ship, Osuna will not think of turning back; he prefers to succumb proudly on the high seas, deaf to the lamentations and clamour of those who go down with him, as he wraps his white cape of Calatrava, like another sail, more closely about him.

The Osuna patrimony was already somewhat diminished when it reached Don Mariano's hands. His holdings were managed by an administrative council composed of five or more of the most able financiers, among them the famous ex-minister, González Romero. Alarmed by the prolonged orgy of spending, they finally prevailed upon the Duke, in June of 1856, while he was in London, to issue an order restricting the admission of further employés. And in 1860, hounded by his creditors in Antwerp, and threatened with imminent bankruptcy, he accepted the resignation of his agents, Don Pedro Herrero and the Marquis of Alcañices, and named the celebrated Bravo Murillo his general agent.

But it is said that "as we grow older we become both madder and saner," and this was, no doubt, the reason why, when Bravo Murillo, after an exhaustive study, offered to balance his budget and save him from ruin in a few years if he would only moderate his expenses, the Duke refused to change his luxurious style of living in the least detail.

It is told of him that whenever he left the house a tray covered with gold pieces was set before him, from which he took several of the coins and left the rest. He would never examine a bill or an account.

He was like the winding Horn of Plenty, where nothing stops, and nothing can retrace its course. "Exuberance is beauty," said William Blake, an infernal phrase.

The true dandy does not need money. "Unlimited credit is enough," said Baudelaire. Osuna resorted to loans, because in reality his prestige was not based on his fortune but on his credit.

He refused to see his ruin; strictly speaking, his dandy's code prevented him from seeing it. For the characteristic of the dandy "is that aloof air which comes from his unalterable determination to let nothing disturb him," or "the pleasure of causing surprise and the pride of never being surprised." And because he was, and wanted to be different, he kept people at a distance with his over-polite affability which, while exaggerating courtesy and ceremony, merely emphasized his invincible disdain.

In March of 1870 Merimée met Osuna in Cannes. He had not seen him in fifteen years. Osuna was obese and deaf. Merimée says he had to shout his head off to make him hear. They discussed the political events that were taking place in Spain: the peasants in Andalusia were not paying a penny of their rent.

Osuna seemed affected by what was taking place, but he displayed "neither indignation nor rancour," and Merimée was struck by the dignity of his attitude compared with the uneasiness of the French emigrés.

XLVII. AT THE SERVICE OF THE REPUBLIC

Quand Neptune veut calmer les tempêtes, ce n'est pas aux flots, c'est aux vents qu'il s'addresse.

RIVAROL

IN Madrid, early in October of 1873, a newspaper published the following lines with a photograph of Osuna: "The name of D. Mariano Téllez-Girón, Duke of Osuna and of the Infantado, Count-Duke of Benavente, and Lord of more titles and patents of nobility than any other Spaniard of the day possesses, would not occur to us, nor would his photograph seem in place, now that all the insignia of rank have been abolished, if it were not owing to the circumstance that he is heading the Spanish delegation of the World's Fair in Vienna." And after enumerating his merits, it concluded: "He has always served his country with the utmost generosity, keeping aloof from the political conflicts of the different parties. A republican government sought him out in his retirement in Belgium because it esteemed his services necessary on this occasion, and he left his castle at Beauraing, where a troublesome nervous disorder keeps him prostrated at times, to go to Vienna and put his prestige and his connections with the imperial house of Austria, through his young and beautiful wife, at the service of the interests of Spain. The *Ilustración Española* takes pleasure in honouring this illustrious patrician in the name of our commerce and industry, which he has honoured."

Osuna went to Vienna where a number of the sovereigns and magnates of Europe and Asia had come together, and remained there, living in his wonted splendour, and attending openings, receptions, competitive contests, and finding a few moments' time to see the curiosities which are a feature of such expositions. Accompanied by the Princess-Duchess, in wheelchairs, followed by footmen, he went from one building to another, tasting a beaker of sherry in the pavilion of Jérez, or admiring new inventions—non-combustible starch, extract of tobacco—going into raptures over a Vestal temple made of tallow, or the

Gothic cathedral which a thread factory had constructed of spools of silk.

Osuna served the Republic even though he visited the Countess of Toledo, the ex-queen of Spain, at the Hotel Britannia; and he served the ideals of democracy, for deep in his soul he carried the hidden instincts of a destructive leveller.

The watchtower of a castle receives no shadow from the flat roofs; only an occasional lofty belfry may vex it. "The Duchess of Guermantes," says one of Proust's commentators, "can go so far as to accept an invitation to the Presidential Palace." Osuna can serve the people, for he was born among them, and embodied all that was aristocratic in them, and to them he returned in the end, with empty hands, poor and ruined. And the people, then, with their curious phantasy, wove him a legend, because it is well known that "in times of peace reputations are made by the upper classes, and in times of revolution, by the lower."

Osuna's reasons for tacitly supporting the revolution were not because of an ideal, as in the case of the Russian princes, or impassioned convictions; nor was it out of necessity—Osuna never accepted emoluments of any sort—as in the case of the blue-blooded aristocrats of the Faubourg who surrounded Napoleon III, making Morny exclaim: *La faim fait sorter les ducs des bois*. Nor was it spite or desperation, like that famous Guzmán who sounded the alarm in the Bastille, and has gone down in history with the soubriquet *Tocsin*. Nor was it shrewd opportunism like that of the gentleman democrats in France between 1789 and 1791 (Noailles, La Rochefoucault, Liancourt, Castellane, Clermont Tonerre) who headed the revolution, and voluntarily offered what they knew would later be taken from them by force. Osuna had nothing left to lose; he lived on his credit, and the people recognized this. Perhaps his friendship for the illustrious Thiers or Fernando Córdoba, Minister of War with Figueras, induced him to accept the post; but what at heart really moved him was this subconscious link with the people.

To the people of Madrid Osuna was a remote, fabulous, legendary figure. He rarely came to the capital. Its provincialism oppressed him, its penury, its lack of refinement. Like Sofia Troubetskoi, who became the Duchess of Sexto, he felt that "Madrid is a zoological garden, with more monkeys than lions."

During his brief visits he was subjected to constant annoyance. He was beset by relatives accusing his agents of dishonesty, who in turn pointed out to him his family's cupidity. And all of them, with rare exceptions, were out to fish in troubled waters. He was hounded and vexed by suits and foreclosures. Everybody was trying to grind his own ax, and creditors, relatives, and agents combined to give Madrid that unpleasant spectacle which, in the pithy phrase attributed to the Duchess Rosario Alba, was known as "the rending of the last tatters."

The Duke of Osuna left no heir of his body. His cousin Uceda, Don Tirso Téllez-Girón, was impatiently claiming the titles and duchies of Osuna, Bejar, Benavente, and Arcos, and had been suing since 1868, to inherit them while Don Mariano was still living. At the same time Don Manuel de Toledo, a natural son of the last Duke of the Infantado, litigated for a long time, and wrested from him, one after another, considerable holdings and the titles of Francavila, Villada, Cenete, until he finally obtained that of Pastrana, and other rich entails with which he was able to keep up palaces like the castle of Henry IV at Pau, where he lived until his death.

His relatives in Italy did their share of pillaging, and the Duchess Leonor went on piling up debt after debt. Hemmed in on all sides he took refuge in Beauraing—*le cœur gros de rancune et de désirs amers*—and decided to wreck the temple and all the Philistines. He took deadly aim and persevered in his intention, for by persevering in madness one achieves wisdom, according to Blake.

At the end of his life Osuna, like another Job, was shattered within, but outwardly his appearance was rich and sumptuous. He needs money. They tell him there is none. He arranges for new loans, and then his administrators begin to lend him money from his own income, charging him exorbitant rates of interest. He has become his own moneylender. The circle is complete. Now he is devouring himself; now he is eternal.

He had little use for history. He left no biographers; Captain Chamorro, in 1857, did nothing more than copy his service record. But the legend saves him, in spite of the historians, who, when they did see him, it was only to disfigure him. This was the case with Don Juan Valera, who mentions him most frequently and at greatest length; this happened with Bethancourt, who plaintively upbraided him, with his timid class-consciousness: "Did the founders of the houses of Ureña, Infantado, and Benavente entail their estates so that one alone of their successors might squander them away in foolish emulation of the Tsars? Did he think, like the last of the Montmorencys in France, that a great race ended with him and that he could take as his motto that famous *après moi le déluge,* of which it is known that Louis XV was not the author? He who was everything, general, ambassador, academician, senator, Knight of the Golden Fleece, thanks, above all, to the name and position he had inherited from his illustrious ancestors—how is it that he never once felt the sacred obligation of looking after him?"

So he would have converted the fiery runaway steed, the angel with its spread wings, the eagle with its motto *Better to fly,* into a pillar of salt? Did not Osuna, the great destroyer of entailments, do more perhaps for the thin-blooded aristocrats by tracing—with smoke, and in the air, but once for all—the ideal figure of a great noble, and delivering it into the hands of the people, thereby rendering it immortal?

XLVIII. GREATNESS AND DECLINE

J'ai rendu de l'éclat, du lustre, des beautés,
Puis, comme a toute chose, il sied que l'homme meure.
Je pars en emportant et laissant des fiertés.
R. DE MONTESQUIOU

THE women in arms once more. Conspiracies are going on at Bedmar's house and at the Duchess of Sexto's Christmas Eve Mass. This lady is none other than Sophie Troubetskoi, Morny's widow, married to Alcañices, the sporting duke, and she lends her powerful support to the gay young blades. Romero Robledo, Ducazcal, and Frascuelo, aided by bull-fighters, picadors, barbers and the rest of the hard-boiled crew that make up the "Brandy Squad" are popularizing Alfonso XII's cause by fair means or foul. The Federals are giving way. But the cause needs a group of ladies to offset the band headed by Maria Bushenthal and the Duchess of Torre.

There is no lack of charming "alfonsinas." The charm of an adolescent king with a winning smile and "come-hither" eyes quickly sowed the symbolic Bourbon flower on every feminine bosom. The most ardent of his supporters were the Marchioness of Torrecilla, the Duchess of Osuna, the Duchess of Gor, the Marchioness of Santa Cruz, the Marchioness of Javalquinto, the Duchess of Bailen, the Marchioness of Molins, the Countess of Sástago, the Marchioness of Miraflores. The "grito de Sagunto" awoke a joyful echo in all these hearts. The King entered Madrid on a white horse. But his triumph cost the Sextos their fortune. The Princess Leonor spends more recklessly than ever. She is among the most active of the ladies; it is said that the king is in love with her.

Osuna returned to Spain as vice-president of the Senate in 1874. The Duchess and he visited Madrid more frequently for brief sojourns. They continued to live in their accustomed style. Their pomp dazzled the new court. The Princess-Duchess is made Countess-Duchess of Benavente on March 8, 1872, and on April 24 Queen Mercedes pins the red bow of Lady-in-Waiting on her.

Osuna outdid himself on the occasion of the royal wedding: carriages of state, fireworks. The more he owed the more he spent. In July of 1878 he contributed with half of the extensive grounds to the establishment of a school for orphans of the war. He spent over $25,000 on a masked ball which he gave during Carnival. The eternal impertinence of the old dandy still persisted when he planned his entertainments. For example, on Christmas Eve he gave a magnificent dinner, followed by a dance. The whole neighbourhood shared the feast through the unshuttered windows. The entertainment was the talk of the town. It cost in the neighbourhood of $30,000, and only twelve couples were invited because the number symbolic of their Majesties who honoured him with their presence, was twelve (Alfonso XII).

This eternal prodigal son scandalized everybody with his extravagances. "Prodigal from lack of will power," wrote Don Francisco Silvela in the appeal to a higher court in the name of Osuna's creditors; but probably not, as he also said, "because of a complete lack of understanding," for the Duke of Osuna went to his ruin fully aware of what he was doing. A newspaper of the day rightly said: "The novel of the Count of Monte Cristo is less improbable than the history of the last Duke of Osuna."

The decision of this gallant musketeer was firm and unwavering . . . *de ne rien garder en s'etant tout donné.* He was the Duke of Osuna, Lord of Morón, and, though stripped of his plumes, he went on crowing, like the cock. He lived the same as always; his pride and pomp blinded him and prevented him from seeing what was going on around him. But anybody who visited the Vistillas palace, like Morel-Fatio in 1876, would have seen that he was plucked bare.

"What a house, sir! And what they have done to it," says an ancient servitor to him, and when the illustrious Hispanist ascends the main stairway, flanked by hunting scenes and the moth-eaten white bear, he sees gaps in the armoury, in the library, and in the coin collections: gaps caused by the rending of the tatters. "The suits of armour of the iron-clad knights on their caparisoned steeds were incomplete: one lacked a helmet, the other a glove or spurs, etc."

But the Duke was oblivious to such details, and because he did not see them, he was still a great gentleman in the hour of his defeat. The tempest cannot engulf him even though it sweeps away his patrimony. A flying eagle or a runaway steed, this Girón will save himself by soaring above the storm, though everything about him goes down to destruction. Osuna never has, never can take thought for the morrow. When, finally, he realizes his situation, and sells his ruin, the Bank of Castile offers him fifty million pesetas for it.

XLIX. RIDING THE GALE

Le dandisme est un soleil couchant . . . superbe sans chaleur et plein de mélancholie.

BAUDELAIRE

PRINCE WILLIAM has not yet grown his classic triangular moustaches. He is not yet the Kaiser. He is not even the heir presumptive, for the Prince Imperial, his father, is still alive. And yet, he has barely changed his white student's cap for the helmet crowned with the gilded eagle, when his histrionic character begins to show itself in a multitude of details.

He is about to be married, and when his fiancée, Princess Victoria Augusta of Schleswig-Holstein makes her entry into Berlin, the Prince vanishes from sight, dashes off to Potsdam, and returns with his company of Grenadiers to render military honours to the astonished Princess just as she is passing through the central arch of the Brandenburg Gate. "The fancy of a prince and a soldier, which reveals the incipient lightning-change artist the future emperor bears within him," is the observation of a writer of the day.

And Ludwig, in a commentary which involuntarily calls to mind the Kantian dove, says of the budding Kaiser: "A raw youth, without preparation, who was swept on to autocracy and arrogance because he failed to meet the necessary resistance in his nation." Neither had Osuna found any resistance, and he had lived on the vain tatters of his hollow shield. And it was precisely Osuna whom Alfonso XII designated to represent him at the wedding, with the rank of Ambassador Extraordinary.

Osuna was always the indispensable ambassador. There was not another decorative figure in the court who, like him, was willing to undertake such missions at his own expense, and with such display and luxury. He could still do things properly—better than anyone else—in spite of being totally ruined. Even more now than ever before, that he was but an empty shell, solemn and impressive, held up by his own pomposity.

Utterly hollow and void, it is now that Osuna, more than ever, is most completely himself.

And he goes off to Berlin, with all the splendour of carriages, liveries, and lackeys. He is accompanied by the beautiful Duchess, for whom the Ambassador-General's adjutants form a small court: the only three colonels at the time who are also Spanish grandees: Ahumada, Sierrabullones, and Valmediano. The latter, who is Admiral of Aragon, wears the red uniform of the Hussars of Pavia. He is the Duke's favourite relative and will inherit the titles of the house of Infantado.

On February 27, 1881, the Spanish delegation sallies forth in all its glory from the Kaiserhof Hotel which the Duke has taken over for the time being. Afterwards they attend a solemn ceremony, at which the two colours which stand out are the white of the gloves and the red eagles. The Spaniards can see nothing but the straight backs of the Teuton princes, with their shaven heads and their two hands clasped on the hilt of their swords. Their faces resemble a bull-dog's, and they wear dark military coats, with the Iron Cross at the throat, and light trousers. Their wives are with them: tall top-knots, stiff collars, high busts, uncompromising corsets, tightly pinioned elbows, feather fans, and long gloves.

Osuna can still gain victories, though he is nearly dead. His courtliness has been such that the old white-whiskered Emperor feels himself under obligation to him. He allows the other delegations to depart, and has the Spanish stay a week longer. He spares no effort to make their stay agreeable, and as there are no more crosses or honours that can be conferred on the Ambassador, as he has them all, he presents him with his own bust in bronze, mounted on one of the cannons captured from the French in the Franco-Prussian War.

And Osuna departs for Beauraing with his trophies. He shuts himself up in his favourite castle, a castle of cards, which he had rebuilt in that fragile mediæval style of the nineteenth century, and which was to last almost exactly as long as he. The Duke loved Beauraing. He had it painted by Legrip in 1863 and again by Perichc, so he could carry the memory of it with him wherever he went. But this was no longer necessary. He had sentenced himself to ostracism in Beauraing, and he was never to leave it again until his death. And the sands were running low.

Besides, he preferred not to return to Spain, because all his patrimony was in the hands of his creditors. In order to unify the debts that threatened to swamp the house and to prevent new foreclosures like those of the year '63, Osuna's agents mortgaged the holdings he had left in Spain, which were evaluated by the Bank of Castile at fifty-four million pesetas. And that same year of 1881, an issue of bonds, covering the debts, which amounted to forty-three million pesetas, was made, signed with a rubber stamp of the Duke's signature.

Osuna had lost again, but his honour, if not his fortune, was saved from the clutches of agents and creditors.

Swollen and almost blind he feels himself growing rigid at the approach of death. And he bows his head and lies down. Slowly and solemnly the sun sets in Beauraing. And little by little Osuna passes to the other life from this which he had lived so splendidly.

Like that Bishop Clermont-Tonnerre, who shone at the court of Louis XIV, Osuna could exclaim with his last breath: *Seigneur, ayez pitié de ma grandeur.*

* * * * *

"Yesterday, on the second of June, 1882, at 6.30 A. M., at his castle in Beauraing, and with all the comforts and ministrations of the Catholic religion, there departed from this life he who at St. Petersburg had dazzled the courts of the Tsars with his splendour and magnificence," the papers wrote.

And afterwards: "The Executive Committee of the Osuna creditors will sell at public auction the palace and gardens known as those of Osuna, etc. . . . The creditors will not be able to realize even thirty cents on the dollar."

And still later: "Today the official gazette exhibits the last tatter of the opulent and powerful Giróns, the rivals of kings, the first among the great nobles, lords of sumptuous palaces and boundless estates: *Sic transit gloria mundi.*"

L. THE PYRE

O haine de Venus! O fatale colère!

RACINE

HERE it comes down the stream. The proud galleon now drifts rudderless and with furled sails. With his white cloak of Calatrava as his winding-sheet, this last Girón returns to Spain.

The Princess Leonor does not cut off her fair locks, on Osuna's death, as did the widow of Morny; but she omits none of the conventional mourning gestures. She orders a portrait of the Duke by Acosta, to match her own. Frapoli, a fashionable sculptor of the day, who lived in Seville, was entrusted with the sarcophagus, which was so sumptuous that when Osuna's remains were carried to Osuna ten yokes of oxen were needed to carry it up to the chapel. But when they got it there it could not go through the narrow door of the pantheon, known as the *De Profundis*. Excess of pomp prevented Don Mariano from reposing with his ancestors. It was taken to the convent of the Immaculate Conception, and there it remained unsepulchred.

The Duchess, who did not receive her allowance, for a month after the Duke's death the Bank of Castile suspended payments, did not pay the sculptor. Time went on. Frapoli grew impatient, and finding his insistence useless, consulted a young lawyer to see if he could evict the corpse! How can he lose the enormous amount of work represented by so much delicate tracery and ornament on a marble tomb where the inscription alone, enumerating honours and titles, has more than two thousand letters?

Meanwhile the Duchess Leonor seeks surcease to her sorrow. She observes that her figure is losing its lines, and she must keep slender. She goes all over Europe searching for ways and means to satisfy her ambitions which know no bounds. At last she discovers something. And on September 22, 1885, at Beauraing, she marries a cousin of hers, His Serene Highness Rudolph Maximilian, Duke of Croy-

Dülmen, Knight of the Golden Fleece, widower of the late Princess Nathalie de Ligne, and the nearest relative of Queen Christine of Spain.

Leonor never loved the Duke. But the storm-tossed Duke always loved Leonor. He felt that there was something perverse in her: *toi qui comme un coup de couteau dans mon cœur—sombre et pourtant lumineuse!* He, who belonged to that type *provocante même dans la froideur,* could not but adore in her the *bête implacable et cruelle—jusqu'a cette froideur par où tu m'es plus belle!*

Osuna made her his heiress in his will "although," he added, "She has done nothing to deserve it."

But, after all, what did he leave her? The most entangled maze of possessions, debts, relatives, creditors, suits, and in the last analysis a shattered fortune, some foreign holdings, a patrimony which had been torn to pieces to satisfy debts to the amount of forty-three million pesetas. Rather than a proof of affection it would seem a subtle act of revenge.

But the Amazon is on the alert once more. While the lawyers in Madrid try to unravel the knotted web, the Princess Leonor shuts herself up in Beauraing, gathering together her possessions, paintings, coin collections, furniture, armour, carriages, jewels, etc.

And one day a raging fire breaks out which envelops Beauraing in voracious flames. Nothing can be done to save it. The castle is ablaze from roof to cellar. The Duchess Leonor manages to escape and takes refuge in Westphalia. But somebody happened to notice through the smoke a blue flame that seemed to run ahead of the fire, as though a treacherous hand had sprinkled kerosene through the palace. It was also said that everything in it was heavily insured, and that the insurance had been collected.

And in a little while all that was left of the magnificent estate was: *Un affreux soleil noir d'ou rayonne la nuit.*

Shadow or light, day or night . . . *Malheur à ceux qui rayonnent,* mourned Lamartine at the death of Count d'Orsay.

* * * * *

God save the Duke of Osuna, the Duke of perils, the valiant Duke, the unblemished Duke, the unalloyed Duke who was consumed in his own brilliance. With its proud banner unfurled to the winds, a life went up in a holocaust to itself. And when the combustion was at its height, the poor sinner could feel how everything impure was burned away, to leave him truly himself, and from the sparks of a puppet, emerged the rigid structure of a soul. Ours is this edifying ruin whereby a man fulfilled his destiny . . . *Il est des pertes triomphantes à l'envi des victoires,* was Montaigne's happy phrase.

THE END